BARKING AT THE HERD:

A MYTHIC MANIFESTO OF THE HEROIC

By Doonvorcannon

1

Cover art by Owen Cyclops

I bark for those who would listen. I bark for those who are meant for much more.

For the few. For the tired. For those looking for a reason and searching for an answer. I bark for you.

Leave the herd.

It begins with a bark and ends with a bite.

With love and power, I present to you this book. May it be of use.

Table of Contents

Preface...5

1: Tyrant...10

2: Godhood Unbound...14

3: The Making of Cerberus (I of III).................18

4: Miseria's Fruit..20

5: Escaping Tartarus..26

6: Heroic Nudity...36

7: An Apocolypse of Sorts: Cerberus Barks (II of III)......43

8: Path of Power...48

9: Of Action 53

10: Sharpened Sword 56

11: The Glorious Desert of the Infinite (III of III) 59

12: The Labors of Hercules..............................65

13: A Few Poems of Power..............................93

14: Eros 95

15: Myth or Not (Rangabes I of III)................100

16: Divine Insanity...110

17: Faith Worth Fighting For 114

18: Men of Greatness 117

19: Feather and Fear (Rangabes II of III)........119

20: Attunded Whole..123

21: Systemic Possession.................................124

22: The Quest for the Golden Fleece...............128

23: Straight From the Source 151

24: The Ironic Oppressor 158

25: Goddess (Rangabes III of III) 161

26: The Sixth Age 164

27: Ascend Olympus 168

Preface

This is a book for the few and not the many. Whether you are a reactionary, a nationalist, or a dissident—none of that matters. What matters is that you have this book in your hands and the fact that you possess such an immortal tome shows that you are on the righteous path of tyranny for tomorrow. The title of this book describes what it is that I set out to do. I am Doonvorcannon; the one that howls and hunts, that bites and claws at the maggots nestled into the rotten flesh of the cult of modernity. Most of the herd has maggots so embedded that to remove such a pestilence requires a natural culling that must and will take place. This culling is non-violent and natural; it is simply the right reception of my bark and the abandonment of the herd for a powerful tyranny that only the freed person can enact. The weak will die out due to an inability and/or desire to procreate sufficiently. They will march off the cliff in due time, barring a stampede-causing event taking place.

I bark at the herd so as to prevent the evil shepherds from bringing us all over the edge, even us righteous tyrants of tomorrow. They want us over the cliff, destroying tradition, culture and nationhood as we know it. This book is for those who would seek power and use it to establish a new tradition that celebrates victory, no matter how immoral the sissy fits claim and shout it to be. I seek to evoke a desire for eternal power that is connected to the blood of the past and future, by exploring and dissecting the heroes of old (both mythical and actual). Some myths give us ways and methods to supplant the current decay wrought by cultural elites. Other myths teach us modern crybabies to man up and seek glory and to never be satisfied.

Satisfaction and comfort are sins, and the two biggest culprits that have led to the worthlessness of mainstream culture and politics as a whole, especially when considering the majority. Victory over vice—what degenerates is what welcomes the abyss. What is beautiful burns with light, dispelling the darkness the vice of the lowly try to curse the victorious with, attempting to force an equality that only drags down the whole into the nothingness.

At times in this book I share my own personal struggles, seeking to help others learn from my mistakes and sufferings. I survived a suicide attempt and learned many lessons of reality from the degenerate nihilism that possessed me as a demon, only three years ago. I want to offer an alternative to the flabby ennui that is swallowing and beginning to digest our society. I don't want to have to rebuild from what is excreted, after the old has been completely dissolved in the stomach acid of greedy individualism. We are not fully submerged in the digestive tract just yet!

This is a book of action, designed to make you want to move with a mythic heroism in mind. I'm trying to recapture the glory of our mythic and heroic past. I'm trying to steer the worthy still trapped in the herd, unto the narrow path of becoming—becoming gods as we were always supposed to be. With this book I want to inspire as many of you as possible to become so heroic and powerful that the mythic is transformed into a final, yes-saying actuality. Say yes to power and drink the cup of poison with glee. Murder your lazy self and resurrect with eternity: Socrates received his death bravely and his ideas became an entity of their own. Drink the cup and taste the burn. If you read this and act, the bitter poison will transmute to the sweetest of honey, and the nectar of the gods will remain at a constant drip into your soul.

A few definitions and clarifications: much of what I say regarding nationalism is within the American system. That doesn't mean the same methods of takeover cannot be applied elsewhere, but for sake of brevity and simplicity I focus mostly on America when discussing the political realm and government. Also, when I refer to tyrants and tyranny I do so positively unless explicitly stated otherwise. To be a tyrant is to tyrannize your own weakness, and to be powerful in everything you do. It is to have a commanding (whether literal or figurative) influence over others too. Nationalism is used as a placeholder for those who want to become a powerful people worthy of the heroic countenance. By nationalism I mean a combination of traditionalism, respecting and seeking power, and caring for your own before anyone else.

The moderns call us Dark Age backwards fools, for they cannot comprehend what it is to seek power and glory in a heroic manner. They see anything honoring the past as a threat to their sissified society that believes greatness is a sin and that weakness is the only good. Light to them is darkness. To them, everything is the opposite of what should be. To one submerged in total darkness, light is as fire is to ice. Yet, to one wrapped in true light, darkness can only pierce such a shroud when eyes are shut. My eyes are open and my gaze is fixed on the heroic, and the brilliant glow of power will dispel the shadows of leftist villainy. Darkness is an absence of light. Where tradition is forgotten and heroism maligned, there is an absence of true power. The power possessed by the elites is perverted and a lie. Their power stems from resentment and weakness. True power is the ultimate good, and it is the source from which all heroism flows. Burn away the shadows of weakness! Burn away the absence of greatness!

There was once a herdsman from Greek mythology known as Actaeon who met an untimely end. His fate was a gruesome one. He was turned into a deer and his own hounds hunted him and tore him to pieces. I want to set the hounds of our system against itself, even if it takes an Actaeon to bring about such change. I'm not calling for violence or a militaristic overthrow; such thinking is pointless and unhelpful in our digital age. I'm calling for using the system against itself, taking positions of power and enacting change until the herd is once more freed to follow greatness. Never forget that even the hunter can become the hunted. This is a comment on infiltration and how democracy can be turned against itself. In Actaeon's myth, he was punished for gazing at Artemis, the virgin goddess of the hunt, while she was naked. She told him not to speak, yet he heard his dogs and he called out to them and was punished. I'm gazing at the naked source of power and beauty that tradition holds, and its allure is kindling my will into a blaze of fiery power. I might be turned into a stag meant to be hunted by our sad little system of cultural decay. I've seen the glory and power of our past, and to not speak on it is to fall in darkness. We must all realize the dangers of seeking glory. The longing for heroism, and admiration of its pure beauty could lead to us being devoured by our own machinations. It is worth it because our age is desperate for a change.

Our age is desperate for real heroes of mythic proportion to arise from out of the shadows and to hurl thunderbolts at the carrions of darkness decaying our culture and nations. So, I have set out to write this book. I've taken much time and risk exposure, but if even just one of you out there becomes worthy of the mythic heroic, I can close my eyes in peace and let the darkness consume me as the torch burns on in your hand. Heroism is at hand! May we go forth as light bearers into the abyss. Tartarus cannot hold us forever. The earth is trembling. The mountains are ready to be climbed. The summits are abandoned. From the top, we can drown the world in the glow of tradition and power. A change is coming, and heroism is required. Become gods and goddesses! Mt. Olympus awaits.

1
Tyrant

I refuse to be an aristocrat of the soul. An aristocrat is a man of inaction who only cares about himself. I am a tyrant of tomorrow, and us tyrants of tomorrow begin our takeover today. If you are fat, eat less. If you are weak, gain strength. There is no room for weakness if one hopes to bring about a new tyranny. Why tyranny? True tyranny is the only way in which the current bashful tyranny can be overthrown. Tyrants of tomorrow do not pretend. They command, and say what they mean. The tyrants of today lie, and backhandedly pay others to destroy their own societies. For true tyranny to rise up, and a nation of power and familial bonds to thrive, we must begin today the practice of tyranny over ourselves. No porn. No excess. Sober minds are minds in control.

Time is the currency we must not waste. Discipline must become our master. While the masses succumb to the void, we shout triumphantly as we carry Sisyphus's boulder to the summit and launch it to the heavens. We will break this cycle of decay, this nihilism that Nietzsche so profoundly declared must be shattered by new men. These new men will ascend the mountain and climb over the decadent carcasses tumbling into the abyss. Master yourself. Command your will. Climb and do not falter.

The black grotesqueness of modernity envelops us, but we know that through the strength of our will we can turn the blackness into light. I begin this book with a triumph of tomorrow, that must begin today. Join me, tyrants of tomorrow! Join me as we climb out from Hades on Cerberus's back, devouring those who are unworthy. The true America is one of manifest destiny. The land once conquered by our ancestors has been handed over to the weak. Let us awaken then, and howl at the black sun we've been cursed to live under. Ascend! Tyrannize yourself and others will follow in your footsteps. You can make your destiny of power manifest, only if you begin today.

It is all so ephemeral! We all die, and for what? Is living for pleasure—and not even too much at that—worth it? What is the point if the void of nothingness threatens to consume everything and make your dung heap of accomplishments null? Hardly new questions, and ones that have been asked by the greatest minds of antiquity. While I have my answer in religion, I do not think that is enough to awaken the world from its slumber. Much of the nihilism today is chicken-neck Christianity's fault. The mystics of old who tyrannized themselves into submission are looked down upon. The inquisition, the crusaders, the Holy Emperors and the conquistadors—men of righteous strength, faith and power, are explained away as an embarrassment to our weak and tolerant age. Even the old Protestants were strong. They came to America with a righteous and powerful Christianity that led to the USA considering herself worthy of conquering savage lands and dominating any heathen and weak peoples in its path.

Without a powerful and triumphant Christianity that does not apologize but revels in its glory and truth, then the religion of today is better off dead. But then, what replaces it? Consumerism. Masturbatory weakness. Tolerance. Shame. Guilt. Decadence. This is the society we are inheriting. Yet, the rise of Donald Trump and his flamboyant shrug at the status quo offers a glimmer of hope. A bright, gold glimmer that does not apologize for success and triumph. In Trump there is much to be exploited. Under the guise of patriotism or perhaps better put as nationalism, we tyrants can begin to climb the ruins of the nihilism of today. As much as it pains me to admit, Christianity at least in America, while ripe for being used as a weapon, is a runt of a dog that is all bark with no bite.

There is a desperate need for a Christianity connected to the powerful tradition of an almighty imperial faith, or even a triumphant one in the sense of the Protestantism that conquered America. Regardless of religion, the nihilism can and must be replaced by tyrants who acknowledge the void and nod, accepting that an end will come but refusing to play privy to that end coming sooner than later. Do not laugh at the void, i.e. do not pretend it is not there. Nothingness is no laughing matter, regardless of what Camus tried to say.

With a will of iron and blood, pay your respects and burn with the passion of life and suffering while struggling and living more than all the decadents of today combined. In this struggle, in our self-overcoming we might just offer a hope to the hopeless. Trump is the beginning. A path has emerged from the filth and slime of corporate politics. Nationalism that puts the American first—that man and woman of European descent who has been forgotten and spat on. Nationalism that decries dual citizenship. Nationalism that celebrates the taming of this wild continent. Nationalism that does not apologize. This kind of movement can and will succeed. Trump has given us a way forward. He has made our collective ascent much more attainable.

I understand that you see through the lies of certain groups. I understand that you see the face of your country changing. The concerns are valid. But when people see your power and command over yourself and others, when you end immigration and promote healthy, traditional families; a European rebirth of the true America doesn't seem so far off. When dual-citizenship is made illegal, Israeli meddling will be made all the more difficult. Putting on an American first mindset and riding the wave of Trump-styled populism might be just enough to awaken the common red-blooded Americans to the power of tyranny that sleeps within their veins.

Unlikely alliances could form. Many progressives are no fans of Israel and all for putting the American people first (however loosely they might define "American people"). They are for things like free education, loan forgiveness, and other genuine populist positions that put the well-being of the citizens first. They aren't for the fattening of the pockets of the corporate slobs at the expense of their own, and we need to learn from such positions. Us nationalists needn't resign ourselves to the whims and desires of Wall Street and Silicon Valley. Nationalism must put the people first. I know quite a few Bernie bros who voted for Trump out of frustration at the corrupt system. The status quo is losing its popularity. Exploit this. There is greatness hidden where one might least expect it to be found.

2
Godhood Unbound

The obvious first step is to master your body and make it as close to a classical Roman and Greek statue of the Gods and Goddesses as possible, always striving to make it submit to your will and vision for it. But we mustn't merely stop there. The power you possess must be demonstrated. Virile youth and beauty must be celebrated. Wear clothes that highlight your prowess. Show your beauty to the decadent, spindly weaklings of the left. Get enough sun. We must take on the guise of gods and goddesses of old. You might be a Hermes and he might be a Thor, but there is room for all the divine strengths of antiquity in this nationalist wave of tyranny we bring.

Even Hades has a place amongst us. If we do not inhabit the underworld and make it submit, who do you think will remain in control of it? As long as we persist in this world, the underworld remains a part of it whether we like it or not. Cocaine. Alcohol. Gang violence. If there are not nationalists taking on the face of Hades, the underworld will belong to the weak. It can submit, just like the rest of this culture can. In a sense, Trump came from the underworld with his prostitutes, gambling, and playmates. But it did not destroy him, it made him stronger and he made it submit and now he uses it to his advantage. Do not neglect such an area. We need a Hades just as much as an Odin or Zeus.

Women—Athena, Hera, Erato. Men need muses. Men need women of power too. Women must not be skeletons but strong and shapely, powerful and feminine. True power for a woman is found in the subtle femininity that can melt the coldest of tyrants. Yet, where are the nationalist Aphrodites? Could it be that I, a religious traditionalist, am advocating for nationalist women to take on the guise of the divine sultry seductress? Aphrodite is the goddess of beauty and sexual love. It is said that her holy harlots seduced many into her cult. I am not suggesting that women sleep around. No, I am instead suggesting that they proudly display their glory. Have I not already declared the need for a nationalist Hades to swim in the sewage of the underworld? Well, we need an Aphrodite to conquer the hearts of the shallow; a role reserved for a select few—for women so beautiful and sexual that no amount of modesty can cover the sheer power of their divine and erotic allure.

These special women must become Aphrodite and take on the role of a celebrity, parading their beauty in a procession of superior aesthetics. Bugmen will fall in line to worship such a power in our deity-starved society. The cult of celebrity will serve as the cults of fertility did with Demeter in antiquity. The changing seasons of today are the winning of minds and souls to the cause of tyranny for tomorrow. Nationalist Aphrodites, let the weak fools burn in your atmosphere. Venus has no moons! Orbiters will not orbit, for they will fear the wrath of your seduction. No, they cannot orbit, but they will worship and heed the words that drip from your honeyed lips. A nationalist Aphrodite can sway public opinion in our sex-crazed modernity more than any prophet or leader ever could. An Aphrodite can turn the entire public into Eros.

Aphrodite's origin myth is a very interesting one. Kronos (the leader of the titans and father of Zeus) castrated Heaven who is also known as Father Sky and Uranus, and his genitals fell into the sea and foamed with the waves. From this foam, golden Aphrodite was born, at least according to Hesiod. Her origin myth offers a key into understanding the inner workings of society, even today—perhaps more so now than ever before. In our current times, I'd call Father Sky the weak and parasitic element that is our corrupt, banker-funded politicians. Father Sky has been castrated by the bankers and goblins that fill his pockets and demand him to do what they say. This castration is all too evident for those who open their eyes, and from that power and corruption a new being has formed. The power of the primordial gods combined with the tenderness of Gaia and the fury of the seas—that is what Aphrodite represents. She is no Hera! She does not nag Zeus and chase him around with weak envy. Aphrodite doesn't need to woo any lovers, she mothered love himself.

Any traditionalist woman reading this who acknowledges the power of the past, do not fall victim to the cult of modesty. Trads are not buttoned up Victorians that purity spiral into the ugly. Some are best suited for motherhood. Some for even an Athena or Artemis-like power that carries an agility and finesse that the masculine struggles with. But for that select few, those Aphrodites who have been told their sexuality is shameful or all they are good for—stand up and smile with red lips and teeth bared. The modern culture is not ready for a nationalist Aphrodite who sings about the old and intoxicates the powerful with otherworldly beauty. Lust is the driving force behind most masculine decisions. It can easily be exploited for good by the right kind of woman.

When I speak of traditionalists, I'm not referring to your old Sunday school teacher who might not have ankles for all you know. I'm speaking about Helen of Troy, a woman beautiful enough to cause a war that even the gods partook in. I'm speaking about Demeter who almost destroyed the world just to have her daughter Persephone back for a few seasons in the year. Or how about the faithful and cunning wife of Odysseus, Penelope? She used her femininity and wit to ward off suitors and keep her family safe until her husband returned, never losing faith in him. Those are the trads I hope you women try to be.

Beautiful, loving and fit. Caring for your own like Demeter. Wielding your allure and luster with power as the lecherous leaders of society bow at your feet.

And Dionysus, I haven't forgotten you, my mad friend! Simply controlling the underworld is not enough. There needs to be more. A lust for living. An earthy and celebratory religion of the now. Thus, we need nationalists whose ranks are teeming with Dionysian men mad with passion and zeal for vitality. Youthful men (and women) who take the cup of wine and drink it, immediately calling—no, demanding for more. I'm not speaking of a Dionysian versus Apollonian juxtaposition here. I want nationalist Apollos to have their moments of madness and passion too! We need our youthful fervor to be so yes-saying, so life-affirming that the dung beetles of the cosmopolitan megacities leave their steaming piles of feces for the grapes of the vine dripping with the dew of vitality that only the Dionysian nationalist possesses. If indulgence occurs, may it be permitted. The poison of the underworld must be brought to the surface, if only to alight the masses with a thirst for a power and purpose that only a greater collectivism and nationalism can truly provide.

3
The Making of Cerberus
Hound of Hades: Part I of III

Cerberus was a small hound. At 3 and a half years old (about 30 human years), he was mangier than most and a mutt in both spirit and body. This was before he took on the name of Cerberus. Then, he was simply called Hound, as if unworthy of any true name. Pups often sniffed around him, chomping at his neck as if intending playful decapitation. Hound did not want to play. He spent time indoors being passively entertained by the colors of the color mirror. His mind gone dormant, he slept through much of his youth.

His parents were legendary monsters. Echidna, his mother, was half-woman half-snake. She was beautiful on her upper half, but terrifying on her lower. She dwelled in Hades and was said to have gotten even more monstrous over time, a hundred heads sprouting from her flesh. Typhon, Hound's father, was even more fearsome. Typhon's parents were Gaia—Mother Earth herself, and the abyss Tartarus where darkness eternally dwelled in misery. Typhon was a serpentine giant who challenged Zeus himself for his throne. Yet Hound spat on his ancestry and power that lied dormant and unexplored in the hollowed caverns of his bones. With safety and comfort as his tombs, he had no desire to honor anyone, not even himself. He was fine with his slow death, and lack of life.

Then one day, a pale god arose from the muck and pointed his scaly finger at the mutt. Hound shivered and hid his face.

"Will you not hear my offer?" he said.

Hound whimpered.

"You lack meaning. You lack purpose. Because of those lacks, you do not live but die. You decay. I can offer to fill those lacks. But you must suffer. You must always exist as a becoming."

Hound shook, but slowly raised his eyes at the god, his mind conquering his tremoring and weak body.

"You must cherish Death, and guard it with all your heart."

Hound wagged his tail.

"Become yourself by honoring your kind. To do them the utmost honor, you must stand at the gates of Hades and chase away any who deem themselves worthy of a bloodhound death. Only those who know they are unworthy will sacrifice. Those who serve their kind must be let through."

Hound barked and nodded his head.

"A bloodhound death is dying for your people, your blood. Come with me and I will show you that you are your people, and that they are you."

The Hound howled as two heads sprouted from his shoulders. Seven living serpents protruded out from his black fur. Cerberus had been born. Hound died in weakness while the new Cerberus prowled at the gate, always keeping out any that were unworthy of glory.

4
Miseria's Fruit

I want to give depression its due, especially in our suicidal age. First, I'd like to share an anecdote from my own life when I struggled much with depression. It was truly a black leash that always pulled and chafed, allowing no freedom or power of the self to flourish in the slightest. There was a lengthy time in my life in which I couldn't convince myself to get out of bed, let alone live. Nothing could convince me of its purpose and meaning when nothingness was all I felt, regardless of my religion. I had become a Christian Nihilist not by choice but by inaction and decay. I was skeletal, weak and sickly and I couldn't convince myself to care. I wept constantly until the tears dried and I was left only with a withered desire to decay. I simply was, and I knew that my "was" would soon become a "never" once I allowed myself to swallow the bilious poison that had been pluming inside my clipped breast. The onyx feathers of suicide had grown inside me for so long that to move at all, to flex my wings, I would have to end myself. My tarred feathers tricked me into seeing no other movement. It was either stay in bed, or act and end it all.

And so, one day in a fit of elation I walked out of my job, gathered a death concoction of pills and alcohol and walked along the highway into the mountains, searching for a nest to die in. The land I dwelt in was too populated and gaudy houses scarred the tree-covered mountains I'd assumed were unblemished and free; I was forced to retreat to my apartment and achieve flight in the confines of my room.

I took hundreds of pills and drank copious amounts of whiskey. I then ran the bathwater and stepped in—in hopes of drowning. My mind was rent into ribbons— tattered sails tossed into the stormy seas as the boat of my body sank fast into madness. I saw people from my past come as ghosts and tell me how I had failed. I saw strangers accuse me quite rightly of being a nobody who was not even capable of cleanly killing myself. My muscles liquidated and I could barely crawl. I'd somehow pulled myself from the now bile-filled bathtub. Voices laughed and cooed from the darkness as my shivering bony form pissed and vomited blood. I dropped 20 pounds in three days. I saw visions of hopeless evil, and visions of a shadowy grandeur that seemed to belong to someone else. That someone else appeared to be a stronger me that had hitherto never existed. The only reason I survived my attempted suicide was because I sent a confused text the third day without quite realizing it. My family came and they were shocked at my P.O.W.-like appearance, with little life left in my sunken carcass that only just managed to move. Like a swatted fly twitching in its own gore, I was still alive in spite of myself.

Somewhat hilariously, just before they came, I'd managed to crawl around in my room as I received a lightning strike of clarity, realizing I couldn't let them see the evidence of my failed suicide. And thus, I hid the evidence well enough, and the hospital I stayed at the next two weeks thought my illness was insect or virus related. I escaped the ridicule and doubt that a failed suicide would undoubtedly have brought about. And my awakening to the heroic, to the mythical had begun.

Oizys, the primordial goddess of misery and depression, better known by her Roman name Miseria, had blessed me with a caustic taste of the bitterest of her truths. Her fiery fruit was cold and black, the sweetest of plums that only tastes ripe in memory, but in the moment of consumption is jagged and bloody. It tears the insides and kills most mortals who taste its scalding, sword-like bite. But to survive and have the memory is to turn all biting pain and bitter darkness into the saccharine—to the honeyed sweetness of always accruing strength through the darkest of horrors and the lightest of mercies.

Miseria has blessed me with the knowledge of final defeat, so nothing can ever truly defeat me again. I say all of this to offer a remedy to the modern prevalence of depression that by no means is foreign to nationalists. With cultural decay and malaise so entrenched, you'd have to be mad not to always be discouraged, yet (and this is a crucial yet)—the decay cannot touch you if you use it to fuel your activity of life-affirming and life-bringing heroism. The mind is more powerful than you think. After eating Miseria's fruit and giving up on it all, my accidental survival opened my eyes to a startling truth: I was only a victim and sufferer because I identified as one. When I shifted my focus and identity (which took a heroic effort that lasted many grueling and still darker months) to that of the heroic—the tyrant that dominates and refuses to be dominated. Once I identified as that I started to win.

Failures were opportunities to accrue strength through the wisdom that can only be gained through experience and learning from said experiences. Depression, addiction, whatever evils assail you: use them. It is a war and in war, everything that goes unused is a missed opportunity. Use your angst and darkness to fuel a special kind of greatness that can only come from such a place of pain. Napoleon in his youth wrote of committing suicide and of his despair at life as it was, yet he continued learning and taking advantage of whatever opportunities presented themselves. He used his weakness and pain to fuel his hunger for power until he could become that power, and continue increasing no matter the situation. It is better to have this darkness, to know it and its powerful temptation to swallow and consume. Most great people throughout history had a piece of this darkness within their soul—some more than others, and some that failed to overcome it—but a light had to be lit if they were to survive and thrive. The negative dark had to be swallowed and digested, used as fuel to create a mythic positive brightness that becomes as a beacon for the heroic. Otherwise the darkness is too much and the person collapses under its weight into a closed loop of fatal negativity that feeds on itself and ends in despair and death.

There will always be the temptation to follow a dark romanticism. I've suffered much from this and still do at times. My heroes used to be not men of power but men of melancholy, men who met no success in their lifetimes and lived in destitution and loneliness before succumbing to ill health or their own miserable, wretched hand. As odd as it might sound, their failed struggles offered me hope that no matter what failures I suffered and miseries I lived through, there'd always be the promise of posthumous success. It was an excuse to settle into mire. I had grown comfortable in my cold. My heroes were not heroes but mortals who failed and were only made immortal by some odd chance of fate that I foolishly thought would happen to me. In the darkest of times, I didn't even care for that. So, after my failed suicide there was little left for me to choose. I could try it again or I could try to salvage the ruins of my existence.

I did not decide overnight, it took many tears and desperate cries to the heavens to come out with a sufficient answer. I decided in an almost natural and accidental way to not turn my suffering into a mythic exercise contained within itself, but to use it. I searched for people in history who used the suffering to become powerful. Not dying in despair but living in power, with the darkness as fuel to be greater. Following their leads, I breathed deeply and thanked the Lord that I had been such a failure that I couldn't even kill myself successfully. An ironic ineptitude that I laugh at fondly, knowing now that the path to power is a long and slinking one with many holes and depths that consume those who meet success too often. My failure was why, and is why I can live and face any failure that scuttles my way.

If you are struggling mentally and/or physically, lacking direction, motivation or purpose, I have some small suggestions that might just help. Don't worry if you don't know where to start in bettering yourself, or if you're so far removed from your goals that you've succumbed to complete inaction. Even if you procured all the self-esteem in the world, you'd still be weak and pathetic without action. It comes down to movement, i.e. progress and not just feeling. If you can coexist with those evil desires to give up by just doing a little something every day, the art of becoming will consume the anxiety and pain of any sclerosis. But don't even waste time thinking about if you can coexist (you can), just begin. Begin right now. Start small. Make your improvement a sacred habit. Read a page a day of a classic. Do a few pushups every other day. Where habit forms, power flourishes.

I used to struggle to read even ten pages a day of some of the denser works of literature. I overcame that struggle by making the habit of reading sacred. I'd make a warm drink and curl up in a nice cozy armchair as I read. Or I'd drink a soothing glass of whiskey while I wrote. The act of first making the drink assured that I would read. Eventually the act of reading became so pleasurable I stopped counting the pages I read because I couldn't, based on how much I was reading. Even as a graduate student with a full-time job I've managed to write this book and read over a hundred books at least, as of writing this sentence. And of course, this is combined with working out. The physical and mental strengthened with a spiritual

desire for glory is the path to eternal tyranny. All three
aspects are necessary.

Returning more specifically to depression, I want to
mention how it can be a strength. It can be a strength when
funneled heroically towards the war of becoming—it is a
battlefield that creates greater heroes because such heroes
know a suffering that most are spared, and they devoured
the suffering, became it and evolved into a greater being
with the potential to always overcome; for to overcome
depression is to be able to overcome all the darkness this
world has to offer. If you suffer from depression, smile and
live; perhaps Miseria will bless you with the sweet taste
and power of the indomitable will of one who refuses
defeat. You can and must become her blessing so as to
bless the world with the strength of a purposeful
nationalism that shines meaning into the darkest corridors
of culture that shun such truth. We are such truth. If you
suffer from depression but continue on, you possess more
of such truth than those who have yet to suffer the
awareness of the decay of inconsequential being. To be
aware of the pointlessness of living inconsequentially is to
be alive Be aware but don't identify as the darkness;
identify as the burning sun that banishes the abyss of black
that has no belonging in the ranks of righteous tyranny. Eat
the fruit and become suffering, so as never to taste defeat
again.

5
Escaping Tartarus

Nationalists in America are like the defeated Titans after the Titanomachy. I say this because they were once so powerful but were thrown into the black abyss of Tartarus. Nationalists were the ones who built this country, whatever they may have called themselves at the time. The founding fathers and great men of our past scowl at the pathetic country we've become. Just as nationalism is thought to be a problematic relic of the past, the Titans were discarded in a similar sense like trash despite birthing the 12 Olympians that took their place. We are still trying to get out of Tartarus; it is a long and arduous climb in darkness so thick that it presses the skin and wraps around us like a suffocating blanket. But progress is being made. To hesitate now, to look back at our prison of comfort just to make sure we can return to those powerless shadows is like Orpheus looking back to make sure Eurydice was still there. Or Lot's wife looking back at Sodom. We'll be stupefied, turned into failures, pillars of salt that are no good for anything but possibly keeping the status quo from rotting. That's what is wrong with the conservatives of today. They seek to preserve some imagined golden age while constantly losing and ceding ground to progressives who want to progress this country into an amorphous blob of milquetoast lacking any distinguishing mark of culture and glory.

We are Titans because Nationalism used to be the normal, just as Titans reigning over the earth was well and good. What changed? When did a Zeus sneak up and destroy cultures of power and tradition? Like Kronos eating his own children out of fear of a usurper arising, powerful nations of old were so fearful of losing their might that they softened their form and allowed the worst to come in.

Rome fell because it allowed non-Romans to call themselves Romans. Invite the rabble in, and your country inevitably becomes the rabble. Of course, all societies have rabble in their lands that cannot simply be eradicated, but they mustn't ever be pandered to like the globalist wrecks of nations do today. Napoleon, for all his faults was a master of defeating and using the mob. The man firing cannons on his own people was one of the tipping points in his rise to power. We need to turn these metaphorical cannons of culture and power on the rabble (speaking non-violently here, of course) to get rid of the ones that weaken the system and burden the strong. A nation is a nation when it cares for its own, and no more than that. America cannot be the savior of the world, which is a foolish, pathetic myth used to excuse all kinds of barbaric acts that are no more than fronts for supporting Israel and getting that oil money. Think about it, if America really cared about the world's well-being and democracy, why is there never any outcry on the news at the acts of genocide and terror almost constantly plaguing Africa? There's no Israel or oil there.

I suggest that all tyrants of tomorrow reading this book take the time to read *Coriolanus* by William Shakespeare. A beautiful and brilliant tale based on true events, it's almost too pertinent to the times we face now in America against these globalist fools.

"...As wars in some sort may be said to be a ravisher, so it cannot be denied [that] peace is a great maker of cuckolds."

What a shame that a man can no longer join the military to fight for his own kind! I commend all those brave enough to serve, but what a travesty that American lives are sacrificed at the altar of Israel. This pretend peace we have strips away manhood and beats tradition into shame. Coriolanus was a brilliant soldier who despised the system of the Roman Republic that gave everyone a voice, even the fools who spoke without knowing what they even meant. He rejected the system and fought for glory. Coriolanus is right in refusing the rabble. He honored a man based on individual merit and value. Not all are worthy of our country. Not all should vote. Democracy as it is today is a farce.

Thinking of the book *Starship Troopers*, I find it intriguing how the government works in this juvenile young adult novel – which at the very least celebrates manhood and sacrifice (something sorely missing in the popular literature of today). In this book, only those who've served in the military can vote and have the right to be called citizens. The thinking goes that only those willing to sacrifice and bleed for their country deserve to have a say in what that country does. I'd be all for this form of government if our military wasn't so corrupted by globalism and serving foreign interests. Yet, what method is best does not matter now, for no voting change in the form of limiting will be enacted any time soon. What can be enforced is proving you are a citizen at the very least.

Why do you think Democrats want voting to be available to the rabble? The rabble votes for weakness, and that is what the party of the jackass stands for.

Coriolanus though is an excellent example of resisting the herd and its lowly barbarism. He was no savage, he enjoyed honor and the finer things of society. Being against democracy does not make one some wool-brained sheep hungry for grass and not caring where or how he gets it; far from it! Coriolanus, the brilliantly talented military man, valued only what was worthy and honorable, much more so than the foolhardy senators and citizens of Rome. *Coriolanus* really is necessary reading for dissidents in our day and age. "Let it be virtuous to be obstinate" and "Manhood is called foolery when it stands /

Against a falling fabric" are quotes that are depressingly pertinent to our own culture of decay.

I tell you that I bark at the herd, hoping to warn some of the deceived citizens of the dangerous and treacherous path they follow. Coriolanus didn't just bark at the herd, he snarled at them. He provoked their resentment and paid the price. May we be provocative, but not to the point of banishment. With the right amount of tact and mirth, we can play the jester that dances to the tune of the herd but whispers against the shepherd. In the end, snarling will get us all killed. I bark from the hills, and I bark from ahead. Sometimes I bark from within. If the herd hears enough barking, from enough different facets of life and station, will they not stop and consider that perhaps the barking has some bite? Do not forget that infiltration is the end game. Nothing is too far gone to be made new. Rome from Empire to Republic, and vice versa. Monarchies to democracies, to dictatorships. Ottoman Empire to secular state, back to a quasi-dictatorship under Erdogan.

Accelerationists are pessimistic nobodies who need to shut up and hide in their vaults while the real shakers and movers get their hands dirty. I have no time for scared men of inaction. Say what you will about Coriolanus and his frank disdain, at least he didn't hide or hope to bring about some destruction (the destruction he brought was forced upon him). He was honest to a fault, and only sought to protect his honor and to wrong the fools in Rome who had ruined his name. May we learn to not be too proud to infiltrate as Coriolanus was, and may we not push our society over the cliff and hope that in the ruins of greatness some tiny sliver of imagined purity could be formed. That is not worth it, if you ask me and I refuse to watch my nation die in the name of some purity spiral unto nothingness. Coriolanus is a pertinent work of literature that we must all learn from.

Interestingly enough, Coriolanus was banned at various times and places because it was thought to be fascist and anti-democratic. At the very least the play makes a case against letting the mob rule. Rome was better with kings. Why should the uneducated and untested vote? Alas, we need to work with the system as is. Do not think for one second that I am taking the classic conservative route of today by holding on to shifting sands that will be lost in time. With nationalism peeking its head out from Tartarus, people have no idea of the might the body of this once glorious Titan possesses.

The hundred-armed Hecatoncheires and the mighty Cyclopes guard the gate, and modernity casts its hazy eye at our ascent... but nationalism is nature, and Heaven and Gaia have reunited, propping up the primordial beings of the beginning, unleashing Chaos and his children. Did you know that Chaos's children consist of Tartarus (our black abyss of imprisonment) and Nyx (goddess of night)? The abyss and night had a child of their own:

"Black-winged Night // Into the bosom of Erebus dark and deep // Laid a wind-born egg, and as the seasons rolled // Forth sprang Love, the longed-for, shining, with wings of gold." -Aristophanes.

Love born from night and the abyss, with chaos as the grandfather. That is what nationalism brings. The powerful, divine love that hatches from suffering and hopelessness is what will come when nationalism leaves Tartarus forever. Eros! With the god of love let loose how can the giants of modernity stay such an eternal, sublime hand? We are in a time of chaos, which is why the stability of nationalism has found success in other countries. America electing Trump is the beginning of a nationalism here, but whoever is elected next must be further right! There are certain thinkers, particularly on the far right and within such circles that think all is lost and that we must prepare for a collapse. They underestimate peoples' love for comfort, and when nationalism is shown to provide the most comfort, security and meaning, then how can it lose? The modern man thinks chaos will not meet him. What such a man fails to see is that his infatuation with modernity is bringing the chaos he despises. Feminists and homosexuals support Islam when such a religion would toss them off a roof or stone them to death.

Demagogues will arise—in truth, they likely will have to if societies are to be turned around. Just as communism and fascism stormed through the last century, a new nationalistic tenor will drown out the pathetic whispers of individualistic capitalism that is based on a meaningless nihilism. A new, mutated Marxist-like capitalism is possible, no doubt, but the suicide epidemic coupled with ennui will be enough to destroy the countries built on greed. It does not hurt to be prepared, but you cannot keep this preparation to yourself; it must extend into the political systems you know and inhabit. Build cultural capital and infiltrate.

When nationalism bursts forth from its cocoon, Tartarus will swallow the lies of individualism because those who are bound together with ties longer than time will stand on a firm foundation of family, while the lonesome bugmen and lardtubs shout and shout as they fall forever in darkness—Chaos swallowing them whole and more effectively than Kronos ever could. Thus, Titans will return to the throne only this time allied with the forces of nature that called them into being. There does not need to be an economic collapse. There does not need to be a world war (and there likely will not be, as mutually assured destruction keeps even the vilest and most selfish minds in check). Remember, even Zeus feared Nyx. So it follows, that even modernity fears tradition. Trump has accelerated not a collapse, but a beginning. The pessimists and nihilists can go hide in their caves and prepare for an end, while the tyrants of tomorrow take power, build culture and create monuments worthy of eternity.]

"So then, there is no point in losing heart, getting upset, complaining. You must close your mouth. Let no one perceive that you are disturbed. Don't fume with anger, as if to work it out of your system, but rather be calm. Burn the devil through patience and forbearance." -Elder Joseph the Hesychast.

"Burn the devil through patience and forbearance." Complaining as catharsis is a waste. As Christ said to his disciples, if they were turned away, they were to simply dust off their feet and know that in the coming times such a city and people would suffer more than could be imagined. Consider such statements in light of the political instead of the spiritual. It does not mean we should take on what Nietzsche called *ressentiment*. We are barking at the herd, not in the herd! All it means is to let the "dead bury themselves" and not waste our efforts on third-wave feminists and the soy boys. They will not last in a proud society. Either their sensitivity will cause them to hang themselves or they'll flee to some progressive utopia that by that time will likely be overrun with third world immigrants hungry to feast on their weakness.

Be patient friends! Many in the herd have never encountered our views and if they have, it was likely through a medium that portrayed us as absolute evil and the worst scum of the earth. Yet if we speak only when we have something of substance to say, and patiently allow the other side to yelp like little dogs while we better our society, do you really doubt that those of the herd who have any honesty will ignore us? Think of the men of power who were elected as literal dictators in a feminized society! We mustn't be angry but be patient, putting on the mask of propriety and hearing out the herd, before barking not out of ferocity and ill will, but barking as a guard dog to warn its master of intruders. When the herd sees that our master is the care for our own nation, and that it isn't disconnected and ephemeral like the fading selfishness of individualism, well... such barking will sound like a choir of angels rejoicing at the souls freed from the herd. Those who stay trapped in the ephemeral face worse prospects of their own doing than we could ever show them, and if they are unwilling to join us, then let them attempt to save themselves in the hell they are headed for. It is the few that form a better whole. The whole follows the strongest. The herd trails the shepherd who offers the easiest way. But when the easy way leads to destruction, the few that see the narrow path to victory will ultimately do away with the wide road to destruction until there is only one way left to go, and that is up.

Speaking of nationalism as a Titan, it makes me think of the Titan's fall in mythology and some of the key figures that brought about such a fall from so great of heights. I'm not going to place all the blame on Zeus, or on Kronos and his mishandling it all, but instead another name comes to mind; that of Prometheus. Yes, the Titan that brought humanity fire and paid the price for it. The Titan that in some mythology created humanity as we know it today. Despite all of this, he played a unique and crucial part in bringing the reign of Kronos and the Titans to an end. Prometheus in my mind is a Judas to his own people. He sold them out for the separate people that would become the gods of Olympus. Do not be a Prometheus. We are Titans, clawing our way back from the depths of Tartarus. Zeus and his band of traitors used trickery and help from the monstrous children of Gaia that Kronos had foolishly thrown back into their prisons after promising to save them.

A world of nationalists that focuses on their own lands and lets each people help their own first, is best. When betrayal comes, when a Prometheus rises to the aid of someone or something else, a change of the guard is forced upon the world and the past nations and alliances suffer for it. I do not respect the myth of Prometheus because he turned first against the Titans, and then against the Gods he aided by propping up humanity. It took Hercules to free him from his punishment. Let's avoid the treachery of the past worlds and myths, no matter how heroic and righteous they may seem—treachery is beneath us. Going to aid other nations at the expense of your own will lead to demise on one side, the other, or both and it is in my view never worth the price required.

Do not forget, George Washington wanted there to be only one party so that the tribalism and factionalism of today wouldn't exist. That monolithic view of America at the time made perfect sense and it must be recaptured. Now, lobbies exist to buy politicians onto one side or the other while continually destroying and weakening the fabric of American culture and society. George should have been our Napoleon, but he was much too humble, and it's sad that we've changed the law for Presidents to fit into term limits. I think that you should be able to run as many times as you want and that elections should be had every 7 years or so— just so that there is time to see if the plans enacted work. Sadly, George's hope that we would stick together and work for only the best and not need party divisions never was quite realized. He couldn't have guessed that his country would be controlled by banks and corporations instead of the people themselves. We've fallen a long way, but there is no reason why another George Washington-like character couldn't rise to the challenge. Who is to say that old George's dreams of a unified America cannot be realized? Why not enact a one-party law? Why not take money out of politics? These ideas are not as far-fetched as they seem. The main issue is that the powers that be would do everything they could to stop such nationalism and truth from ever reaching that point. Yet, it has been done before and will be done again. The tide of nationalism is filled with the reserves of Tartarus—power and tradition stewing inside the cauldron for so long that the steam that arises will scald all those unworthy and send them scurrying into their shadowy lands of culture-starved societies that have no place here, or anywhere that nationalism arises.

6
Heroic Nudity

Bronze Age Pervert (BAP) has the right idea about nudist body builders. Hear me out, there is nothing homo about the human form. The human form when reaching peak performance and perfection is more beautiful and glorious than anything else on this earth. Look at Greco-Roman statues and the art of ancient heroes—they are most always depicted as nude. If they wear any clothing it might just be some minor form of armor draped across bare shoulders, or maybe as headwear. The body is displayed and their godly physiques are exposed front and center. This is a life-affirming action, to display the beauty of the body that was worked for and earned. As hands shape the clay and iron sharpens iron, the chisel of fitness chips away the flaws of flabbiness and fat. Sunned skin wrapping supple muscles that glisten as if of bronze make the weak clothed ones hiding their flaws beneath layers of cloth hunch their shoulders in shame. Kings were portrayed as nude. Gods and Goddesses were portrayed as nude. Now, the modern man feels ashamed to not wear a shirt in public, even if he is fit. I say, rip off your shirt in the most public and inappropriate of places and stand erect as a statue of glory, while the peasants' judgement turns from wrath to a silent awe. Try as they might to feign indifference, the more perfect the shirtless form the more their mortal minds will submit to the god in front of them.

This needn't be limited to men. I might get in trouble for such openness, but I believe that in the same way we need nationalist Aphrodites, we need nationalist nudist women. They do not need to be nudist in the typical sense of the word, but I mean in the sense of the statues and paintings of the goddesses. They do not hide their full breasts and sun-kissed skin. They have no shame about their divine beauty. The beautiful are in sin when hiding away their beauty. It is even more of a sin when nationalist women in the name of traditionalism and modesty hide away their divinity, shielding their femininity as if it were a curse. It is a curse on us all if such beauty is locked away. The same way I go about my life shirtless as much as possible, I ask you brave, Aphrodite-worthy nationalist women to let your flesh sing in the breeze. Feel the loving caress of Helios. Breasts not bound in chains of cloth. Skin not tented as if the sun were an enemy. People of the sun need to let their skin drink as much of it as possible. Become golden and bronze, and if of the fairest skin type, protect it with oils but do not neglect to let it shine like moonlight in the heat of day.

Helios loves our beauty as long as he can see and touch it. Now what I am not saying is for women to run around naked (though that might cause the leftists some confusion once they realize the women are not hairy, fat ugly feminists but Aphrodites so beautiful and powerful that they step on the bugpeople around them with rapturous roars of glory and pride of their people, myth and nation). Propriety is not always an evil word. But when in private, clothes should be kept to a minimum, even if at the moment you are unsightly—keeping yourself sparsely clothed forces you to notice the problem. Man and wife should visit nature in their natural state, nothing separating them in the beauty and power of nature as it is. I'd almost go as far as saying that a true powerful and spiritual experience and knowledge of nature requires nudity, but that is an aside.

Man and woman need to celebrate youthful beauty and sexuality by displaying it and not hiding it. Repressing beauty leads to degeneracy hidden away. Celebrating beauty promotes well-being of the collective whole as more people strive to look good. Monogamy is increased when beautiful couples live together in the open with happiness and pride in their combined beauty. The beauty of a handsome man and alluring woman together I believe to be the highest form of beauty there is. The promise of future beauty from their seed, and the glory of their combined beauty, borders on the divine.

We are sadly not even close to the state of embracing a public-wide nudity project, that much is true. But wearing thin clothing in public, and showing as much as possible without offending local laws should be required of the beautiful men and women, and it should be the goal of all nationalists to reach such a state in which displaying the body provokes the same adulation and silence that Michelangelo's sculptures might. This is not promiscuity or dressing slutty. You can show much skin and still look elegant while doing it (you can do that while in the nude, perhaps even more so if carrying yourself regally but many people struggle with such a conception). People who live in hot, coastal climates are not called slutty when waltzing around in bikini tops and shirtless. I believe that when it is hot, even in unexpected places such clothing could be worn, and if the beautiful nationalists donning such revealing clothes carry themselves regally and confidently, the peasants will bow and make way.

The Wim Hof method of keeping warm works and I suggest researching and learning it as soon as possible. It comes down to being as simple as embracing the cold and not fighting it with shivers and/or hugging yourself for warmth. Do not shiver, but welcome the cold and don't fight it. You'd be surprised how effective such a simple method is. I've tried it many times during winter, while it is 30 degrees Fahrenheit and bugpeople shiver in their carapaces around me as I stride confidently through their midst with my arms bare and my thighs exposed. It is a powerful thing to walk into a room with shivering, wrapped up lardtubs that stare at you in awe as you calmly stride

through their jiggling midst. Muscles unbound in the pallid
winter sunlight take on a glow of their own that seem to
melt the ice surrounding them. The uncovered long legs of
a nationalist goddess, dancing as if on fire and pirouetting
through the cold with naked delight, making the frozen
ones melt with envy. Try it. To be strong, beautiful and
exposed in the winter is to become Helios. We need to
continue becoming always more beautiful and when a
certain level is achieved, that glorious beauty must be
unveiled and celebrated. Beauty is not meant to be hidden,
if unseen it is useless to possess.

A very good scholar frog who is quite **sardonic**
taught me an interesting word: πάγγυμνος (pángymnos).
The scholar frog says it means very, very naked. This is not
simple nudity. *Pángymnos* is the triumphant nudity that
exults in its beauty and power. The female and male can
share in this nudity; it is the only nudity that a tyrant must
possess. Nudity that is for the bath is not what I mean. This
is the nudity of classical triumph. Heroic nudity is
everywhere in art from Ancient Greece, Rome and even
during the Renaissance in Christianity. The gods are naked.
The heroes are naked. The beautiful naked form is heroic
when displayed amongst others, only if that form is worthy
of depiction. To be very, very naked is to walk in the
strength of ascendant humanity. The unfit should always
wear at least seven layers of clothing when in the presence
of others. No beauty should mean no nudity.

To be πάγγυμνος is to let your skin smile back at the
grinning sun—it is to fight uncovered, showing you have
no weakness or fear. It is a nudity reveled in. It is to put
skin in the game. Helios wants to caress and entreat worthy
skin. Become beautiful first. Do not be Narcissus and only
gaze at yourself and not share your beauty with others.
Even worse is to hide your own beauty away to the point
where you forget it exists. In a way, we all hide our beauty

away by ignoring potentialities and refusing to refine ourselves in the fire of struggle. Become beautiful. Display your power. Remove your shirt in a busy area. Watch as the bugs crawl and the lards jiggle with screams. One day, you might reach a level of beauty that causes absolute silence as the bugs transform to wolves licking their chops. You might be devoured by lust, your body ripped apart as the wolves taste the power of perfect nature. With your sacrifice at the altar of perfect beauty, the wolves might just become the moon, and in their reflection of your sunlight, the truth of beauty will force them all to burn in the passionate heat of the incandescent light of nationalism.

And for Christians who are worried about modesty, and therefore covering themselves in shame and imagined reverence – have you forgotten that Adam and Eve were naked before the fall? Their clothes were a punishment! Christ made up for the fall on the cross, so why do we still wrap ourselves like Eskimos in layer after layer of unnecessary and bothersome cloth? Your virtue-signaling with your modesty is just as bad as the left, who love to virtue-signal by celebrating degeneracy. It is not degenerate to show the human form. Have we all forgotten the times in ancient Greece where men did all sports in the nude? Let the little clothing you wear be adornments worthy of heavenly splendor. Do not be ashamed of beauty. Display your God-given natural form with thanksgiving. We are made in His image. The world is already being redeemed. Let us help with such a redemption by showing the human body to others as it is supposed to be.

I understand that one cannot simply walk about in the nude in modern society (though nothing but bodily shame and weakness is preventing you from doing so in the confines of your own home!). However, there is a recent trend among the celebrities that I approve of, and will undoubtedly catch some flak for agreeing with. I'm talking about the trend over the last couple of years to wear see-through tops and forgo bras. I'm not talking literal transparency like a window, but more of something that delicately hints at the powerful beauty beneath. Kendall Jenner is probably the most famous example of this, and she pulls off the look in such a way as to look sophisticated and not trashy. If men can walk around baring toned chests, tell me why women should not? It is a shame that the robes of Ancient Greece and Rome have fallen out of favor. Look at one of those statues and admire how the chest is often bared, female and male alike. There is an excellent statue of Alexander the Great that reveals this look quite stunningly.

Why wear undergarments when nobody can see? If for support because you are naturally endowed, forgive me as I am sympathetic to such a case, but for those like say a Rihanna or Kendall Jenner, display your toned frame and youthful breasts. They will not remain upright forever! What does Socrates say but, "No citizen has a right to be an amateur in the matter of physical training…what a disgrace it is for a man to grow old without ever seeing the beauty and strength of which his body is capable." A disgrace it is, but not just to not know of his or her own beauty, but to not share it with the world! A beauty unique to yourself and your own youth can never be regained once lost to old age. Do not make the mistake of not letting others know what you possess. This does not mean being a thot! This does not mean being vain! We need to drop the Victorian mindset and embrace the Mediterranean one that celebrates beauty and does not call it shameful. Your sculpted form is not shameful. It is meant to be portrayed in timeless sculptures and art for future generations to see and be inspired and encouraged by. I think much of this modesty of today can be traced back through the Puritans and their misunderstanding of Paul speaking of biblical modesty. He was talking about adornments and attire that made one look

like a prostitute. Do not tell me a beautiful model with the
shape of her breasts hinted at under fine cloth is dressed
like a prostitute! Not a prostitute, but a goddess.

This translucent clothing can be worn quite
powerfully by men. I have certain Henley shirts that hug
my muscles and show my statuesque physique in a manly
way, but not all that different from what I mentioned with
the feminine form. For men it is easy, just wear tight shirts
and short shorts. This is not homo, but powerful! Beowulf
fought the sea monster with his comrade in the nude, to
avoid unnecessary hinderance. Metaphorically, the way in
which Hercules was required by Hades to not use any of his
weapons against Cerberus is similar to the naked
Olympians putting their "skin in the game", not hiding
behind weapons and armor. May we embrace our power
and make the virgin bugmen shudder in their slumped,
sissy fit physiques, softer and weaker than us men of power
were even at birth!

7
An Apocalypse of Sorts: Cerberus Barks
Hound of Hades: Part II of III

The crowd trembled in line, quivering like the shaft of an arrow that had struck the bullseye full-force. They all approached a cliff that dropped off into a black abyss. They were spiritually dead; Apollo had long ago shot each and every one of them with his immortal bow and they hadn't even noticed they'd been struck. Eros had fled these vagrants, aware that his saccharine arrow was unable to pierce the crowd's stony, bitter hearts.

"Rabble, turn back if you want to survive the eschaton. Turn back if you want your life to mean something," said a man with a squared jaw and gourd-shaped head. His voice was the epitome of average. It was so banal he could put animals to sleep with his speech due to an absolute lack of any remarkability. His tone and pitch did not match the fervor the words themselves deserved.

"Rabble! Rabble! He calls us rabble but is incapable of believing in we, the good people. Speak for yourself," a fat man slurred, drunk with a six-pack of beer in one hand and a bag of potato chips in the other.

"Have you forgotten? 'Good and upstanding people must be persuaded by gentle means. The rabble must be moved by terror.' The Emperor was right, but in the end, he couldn't help becoming a man of the rabble himself. His terror was his own. Goodness is earned," the square-jawed one warned.

"None of us are Napoleon. None of us want to be, even at the height of his glory. We are happy in our comforts. We don't need meaning. We don't need your promise of power and purpose. And how are you, pathetic man that you are, going to bring terror to us? Why, we ought to arrest you right here!" a mousy-haired woman squeaked, shaking her fist angrily at the sky as if directing her wrath at god and not the square-jawed man.

"Next!" the Executioner shouted, doing a little jig and thrusting his feet over the precipice before pulling them back tantalizingly. The crowd guffawed, oohing and aahing at the spectacle with ecstatic bliss.

The Executioner was a tiny man wearing a black boulder hat instead of the more traditional hood, which made him pleasant to look at. There was something off about him though. His eyes were two little specks of coal that held no hope and spark in them. He looked as if he had checked out long ago, mentally dying and instinctively continuing in only the materialistic sense.

"Step up! Step up! Those who do not follow will be alone. Do you want to be alone? Of course not, my fine upstanding citizens, you only want what is right, what we all know to be right. That's why we read the same books, teach the same topics, and cover the same news. We are all the same!" The Executioner held out his tiny hand and a fat woman and her twig-like husband kissed the hand that beckoned, and smiled as they fell together off the cliff into the blackness. "Next, next! We are making great progress my good people. Progression is to trust in what goes against tradition! Leave the bigotry behind and join together in the warmth of blanketing darkness that forever blots out our evil, so-called differences. When all cannot see, equality is what you bleed. Proceed! Proceed!"

The square-jawed man grimaced, and gnawed his lower lip. Someone shoved him from behind and with his head hung low he joined the throbbing masses once again. Then like a thunder-clap, like a bomb bursting in every individual's eardrums, an eternal bark sounded from the abyss. A bright blue light flashed in the chasm, and a monstrous beast with three dog heads and seven serpent tails leapt into the crowd. The dog known as Cerberus had come, twice the size of even the largest man there. He snarled and snapped his teeth. His serpents hissed, and he leaned forward and bit the little Executioner's head off. No blood spurted out from the neck, but instead rainbow-colored confetti shot out from him like a cannon. The people stared in admiration and cheered, giving Cerberus no attention.

"What a trick!" the fat one yelled in between shoving handfuls of chips down his gullet.

"Brilliant! Amazing how he could control such a mangy mutt," the mousy women hissed, spraying spittle at the Hound of Hades.

Cerberus howled into the empty and gray sky that hung over them like the promise of death, and it instantly blackened with swirling and thick clouds which somehow cheered up the raucous crowd even more. Several of them with rapture threw themselves off the cliff, squealing with delight the whole way until their voices finally faded, long after their bodies had disappeared into the darkness. Cerberus barked at the heavens again, and the sky ripened to a bright orange and red flames burst forth from the glowing clouds like streaks of lightning.

The crowd became even more jovial, and they laughed and laughed as they rolled over themselves to join together as one in the abyss that was quickly becoming a mass grave. The flames from the sky stretched down somehow tenderly, like a mother's arms beckoning her children to safety. These flames purified, they destroyed the unworthy but welcomed the repentant—the rebellious ones who knew that progress in the modern sense would lead to their dooms. The square-jawed man was the first to be licked by the heavenly flames. When the red glow dissipated, he wore a large purple crown and carried a sword made of diamond. The mob, the aptly named rabble, lost their joy once they saw this rebellion, and they lashed out, clawing at the man with harpy-like talons.

Cerberus watched, barking encouragement but standing aside. The square-jawed king cut through the rabble like ribbons. Bloodied and injured, he smiled as he finally understood that he was finally living. Cerberus lowered his three heads in a bow, and the king pet and hugged him. The rabble shrieked but they did not try to attack, at least not physically, now that the king stood with Cerberus. Cerberus barked and the king nodded, then walked away from the rabble and back towards the ruins the progress of the majority had left behind. The king let out a triumphant yell, his voice no longer insignificant but assured and eternal.

More flames descended and only an exceptional few broke away, garbed in royal attire as they went back to reclaim the ruins and make whole the society they'd left to rot. The bones remained and it was up to these royals to breath sinew, tendons, muscle and flesh back into the ruins to make them better than they'd ever been, even at their very best.

Harpies suddenly darkened the sky, their talons clutching at the clouds like a volt of vultures trying to roost in branchless trees. Zeus had sent them, they served as his hounds. The feminine birds cackled curses at the royal ones. They swam through the air, their mottled, feathered wings like monstrous gray oars, and they hurtled at Cerberus. Their venomous beaks dripped toxic tendrils of sickly blue fire, and Cerberus bounded out of the way of their shrieking attacks. He barked into the air and Hades listened, sending reinforcements of his own. Pale green horses of crackling lightning thundered out from the clouds, breathing bright green flames at the harpies. The harpies and horses battled in the sky, and Cerberus stretched his three heads as high as he could and breathed red flames into the sky, using his serpents to bite and bring down as many of the screaming harpies as possible. All the while, the rabble continued leaping into the grave with smiles on their faces and heads down to avoid looking too close at the reality of the situation.

[The headless Executioner went back to his dancing and the rabble clapped along. Cerberus kept barking and fighting, and many kings and queens left the weak to join him in power. But the fight remains unfinished, and Cerberus will keep barking as long as there is some hope that an exceptional few might turn away from the herd of death and become tyrants of life. Hades could deal with the rest, locking the fearful in cages they'd constructed for themselves. But the fight for life was above the darkness, and Cerberus would guard this abyss, this unnatural tomb with all of his faith and power. The hound barks, but only the heroes listen.]

8
Path of Power

I see an amaranthine city with eternal inhabitants encased in marble and stone—statues more alive than most city dwellers today. I see timeless cities being brought to life with classical glory coursing through the streets like the lifeblood of triumphant ancestors returned. That is the future I am fighting for, and the future I want all of you to fight for. The humanless cities of today are built for utility, built for pride, and built for consumption. Mechanized roads wide and desolate blot out the craftsman. The shopkeeper is nowhere to be found. All the while, the globalist companies and higher-ups eat up every square inch that isn't "diversified" while demanding diversity everywhere else but around them.

Nothing being said is new. People realize there is a lack of beauty; this is evident by the vapidity of the vacuous mainstream media, the rampant suicides, and the drug epidemic. To loosen this infernal chain, one must have the cuffs tear at the wrists for so long that one's own blood allows for enough lubrication to slip free. The ancient Greeks believed that volcanoes erupted because a monster deep within the mountain was trying to break free. We are those monsters, and we are shaking the foundations of the mountain so hard that an eruption of any sort has Pompeii-like potential.

We want our freedom from the prisons beneath the mountain. Once free, our ideas will be so powerful and splendent that any sane person will not be able to tear their eyes away from such transcendent beauty. Once the fear of ridicule is burnt out by the increased normalization of our ideas, the people will follow truth because truth is most beautiful of all.

49

We live in a world starved of beauty. Nationalists care about beauty because nationalists care about their people. Every other political movement is based in securing the best for the individual, everyone else be damned. A family that stands together is worth more than an infinite amount of discordant individualists. As a collective we paradoxically become the highest individual, exceeding the caliber even of mighty Zeus. The individuals that want to be alone in their decadence are mere rats. We are a flight of birds of prey.

We are birds of prey, but we've forgotten the heroic taste of blood. Heroism requires blood—your own blood sacrificed and a care for the blood of your people. I read of great and powerful men of history: Alexander, Augustus, and Napoleon to name a few. I read of them and wonder how it is that we've fallen so far from such heroism. It's as if they were gods, not real but made-up. We are all so weak and inadequate that the triumphant deeds of great men are sneered at as if their eternal successes were evil.

Even our fiction is lacking. The superheroes (the serious ones) do not even kill the bad guys. Epic battles and war are treated as an unfortunate backdrop and calamity of savage barbarism. At the very least, our heroes (both fictional and real) of today are not ones that will be remembered centuries from now, or perhaps even mere decades. Pick up any Greek or Roman mythology; read *Beowulf* or any Shakespearean tragedy. I read of these epic tales of overcoming and masculinity, and mourn the lack of both in myself and our culture. Our version of tragedy in terms of catharsis, is watching a bunch of rich black men play sports with no promise of death or risk. They are millionaires! They are not willing to die! Yet the fans of these sports live and die for these millionaires who do not care about the fat patrons watching, as long as they continue paying.

Where are our gladiators? In America, death is hidden away and treated as a shame—robbed of any glory and meaning. Think of a Samurai killing himself for honor. Think of duels to the death because one felt slighted. Brutus and Titinius killed themselves rather than live as chattel. Almost all are chattel today and they prefer it that way. What does honor mean when people celebrate the conformity of buying and partaking in useless wastes of capital, and shun the few good warriors in the military as pariahs? I read *Beowulf* and long for the times when violence was a good and it was gloried in with fitting revelry, while not sugar coating the brutality of it. Read *The Aeneid* by Virgil. He paints both a grim and realistic picture of battle, while also reveling in and celebrating manly triumph and violent overcoming.

The feminization of what was once our Manifest Destiny, our believing and conquering people, cannot be solely laid at the feet of Christianity. Christ never told soldiers to stop fighting and the Old Testament is filled with God ordained wars and slaughter. Turning the other cheek only works in a high-trust society that is homogenous and working as one for the whole. That is what Christ meant when he spoke that commandment specifically to his apostles. The blame is all of ours. I'm aware of the powers in control that want our ancestry to be forgotten and shunned, but we can only blame them for so long. Read Ernst Jünger's *On Pain* and tell me how we experience pain in modernity. We don't! There is some kind of drug for everything, but there is yet to be a drug to match the glory of heroism. To embrace the heroic, the true living people must always be in touch with pain and seek to master it through a will to power that soars in the heavens of heroism. To be heroic, one must always be in pain—pain for yourself, pain for your people, and pain at not achieving more glory.

How can we become heroes today when violence and power are paradoxically viewed as weak? Do we seek combat? It is a good sign that MMA has grown so popular but it is also discouraging because fans will end up treating fighters like their favorite teams; such a mode as that isn't participatory and it weakens the will of a man who cheers for the violence of someone else without ever putting any skin in the game. The heroic requires suffering and risk. The heroic requires the constant threat of death. We can bring about our own smaller deaths every day we choose the difficult over the comfortable.

We hide away our dead and pretend that death is merely an abstraction. Death must be earned in the concrete. Death must be sought after through the glory of violent living. To violently live is to die purposefully. Yet, how can the modern-day man achieve such glory? One must cultivate mastery of the self through the searing pain of always chasing discomfort Nietzsche said it best: "The secret of realizing the greatest fruitfulness and the greatest enjoyment of existence is: to live dangerously! Build your cities on the slopes of Vesuvius!"

So we master ourselves, but then what? Jack Donovan recommends you find your tribe. He isn't wrong but it cannot stop there. How can a man of our time become a Napoleon and turn the Republic into an Empire? It once again comes down to infiltration. Invade the parties, speak the truth, and always be ready with gun in hand. When we nationalists have taken control, the opportunity for a glorious and violent death is certain. In the meantime, if not an infiltrator, at the very least I think you should seek other right-wing radicals and join forces. Act together and destroy communist protestors through patient combat, allowing their limp hands to strike first. We cannot be physically violent in the streets as all the major forces are against us for the moment. We must act with the utmost honor, and train for the day when such an honor will be celebrated and tested. We must bring back the mythical ages of dying divinely for your country. Until then, heroism comes through infiltration.

The myth of Callisto is a perfect example of infiltration and subterfuge by none other than Zeus himself. Zeus disguised himself as Artemis to trick the nymph Callisto into coming into his arms, and he seduced her. The parallels should be obvious here. We as Zeus can disguise ourselves as Artemis to woo an unexpecting government into our arms. Artemis is the goddess of chastity, and her purity seduced Callisto into a false sense of security and trust. It was Zeus who used the guise of the unthreatening system (Callisto was a follower of Artemis) to trick his opponent into ceding power. Can we not do the same? Many a lobbyist has bought out so-called nationalists. As soon as these nationalists receive the slightest bit of power and respect, they bog themselves into the swamp as a useless compromiser who never believed in our lofty ideals in the first place.

That is not infiltration. We all need to support those who receive no booster money (as rare as that is nowadays) and are strong on immigration. That is at least a starting point. But we need to have our middle and end, and that can only be met with a one-party ethos that is unabashed at proclaiming the nonsense of forced equality. Hierarchy and power should be the pillars of our movement. We need to win goodwill and trust and when the opportunity presents itself, make sure you're a Napoleon and not a Robespierre. The latter revolted in nihilistic bloodshed and the former became emperor. Do not forget, those who read this book are already on the path of becoming a tyrant. We need enough tyrants of tomorrow to produce hundreds of Napoleons, each one an emperor of his own state.

9
Of Action

I implore everyone who is reading this to work out. Even if you are busy and hard-pressed, you can still make the time. One, it will make you feel better (endorphins and an increase in health), and two, you will look better, and if you look better you really do feel better, I can attest to that. I think this needs to be stated frankly: you cannot call yourself a nationalist if you are fat and/or weak. Call yourself one once you get fit, and not before. How can you purport to care about your nation and people when you cannot care enough about yourself to work out for a little each day? I'm not talking about body building and running hundreds of miles, I'm talking about simple body resistance workouts that are free and easy. Once you reach a certain point, then you can add the more advanced and difficult stuff, but starting out is the hardest part. I promise you that when you first see those gains and develop a habit, you'll never go back.

Start by doing a few pushups a day. That is what I did. I slowly increased the amount, and now all I do is 300 pushups every other day. That's it. Of course, I do it with 60 pounds strapped on me with weighted vest and on a steep slope, but it only took me half a year to get to that point, and the gains have paid off. I've gained about 25 pounds of muscle doing nothing but pushups. This is coming from someone who has been a twig for his whole life, weighing the same as I did in middle school till just before I started working out. It's not the exercise so much as it is finding something that you don't mind doing and know you will continue to do (just make sure it is difficult and challenging enough to help you gain strength). Consistency is everything when getting started and when pushing through plateaus. And to lose weight, eat on a calorie deficit, no matter how small the deficit is, just make sure to always be on a deficit. If you cut out snacks and only eat when you're hungry you'll be stunned with how quickly you lose weight.

These are not difficult goals. Let us present our best selves to a public that is always trying to malign us. There is no excuse to not be at least fit, or better yet cut. Confidence comes from this, and you will attract better people into your circles. If you take away only one thing from this book, take the importance of fitness for nationalism. Obesity is a sin that religious people seem to have forgotten is wrong. It is evil to wreck the temple that is your body. Don't wear clothes in the privacy of your home and you will eat less if you see blubber, or you will eat more if you see bones.

The Anime One-punch Man is kind of on to something (satirical as it is) with his super-powered and simple workout routine. Just do 100 sit-ups and pushups a day as well as 100 squats. All bodyweight. The only difficult part is if your cardio is bad. Running 6.2 miles a day isn't easy. I don't do much cardio myself, but it is something I need work on adding more of. I do walk a lot, and get cardio somewhat naturally. Also, a fun little tip: dance in between sets. Nietzsche said that "I would believe only in a God that knows how to dance." He danced daily and took long walks. The physical is absolutely necessary for mental clarity and strength. So dance! Walk! It isn't so hard. And try listening to classical music while working out—it is magical. It transforms exercise into a dance with the cosmos. It turns the pumping blood into the thunderous roar of continuous gunfire. It transfigures your mind into a burning torch—thoughts to ash as you become action. I prefer Wagner and his triumphant music but any thumos-producing composer should do fine. Try it out to taste the power of the infinite!

Thomas Jefferson said that a man should exercise at least 2 hours a day, no matter the weather. He actually encouraged seeking out strenuous elements as he thought the harsher the climate the stronger the man would become, like a beast adapted to the tundra or the poisonous, steamy jungle. Ben Franklin also agreed with exposing oneself to the elements. He would take what he called "air baths" in the frigid cold while completely naked. For us, we can do that or better yet, take cold showers. Even if the physical benefits were not that great, the mental clarity and sharpening of your will to intentionally seek discomfort the first thing in the morning makes you strong. Even the founding fathers knew this, and they were not physically strong men in the traditional sense by any means.

10
Sharpened Sword

There is a risk in celebrating beauty to the point of encouraging vanity. By all means, be proud of hard-fought gains, but do not become vain! All one has to look at is the example of Cassiopeia (one among countless tales of vanity causing immense and deserved suffering). She was boastful of both her and her daughter Andromeda's beauty to the point of insulting the gods. Her vanity would not go unpunished, and Poseidon sent the sea monster Cetus to wreak havoc on the country. If not for Cassiopeia's audacity in claiming she was just as beautiful if not more so than the gods, none of it would have happened. The only way to appease the giant monster was for Cassiopeia to sacrifice Andromeda to Cetus. The great hero Perseus ended up slaying the monster instead, saving Andromeda from death and then marrying her.

The moral of this myth is obvious for individuals, but on the macro scale, we can learn not to brazenly challenge the gods without respect. Such hubris and vanity will only bring ruin. We need to become worthy of being a hero like Perseus, slaying the serpent of modernity and turning our horrified foes into stones of petrification. Sea monsters can be vanquished and Medusas decapitated and used for our own gain, but we must never allow ourselves to become so vain that we refuse to engage in anything for sake of appearances (e.g. "politics are evil and I am too pure for such slime"). To purity spiral is to be as vain as Cassiopeia. But who are our modern gods that we mustn't think we are too good for or better than? The answer is our ancestors and powerful cultures of the past. We mustn't think we are too good for religion, or certain kinds of art and architecture, etc. We are not more beautiful than our past, but we are striving to become beautiful in our own, tradition-honoring way.

To honor tradition and the metapolitics of power, we need to be prepared to always have an answer at hand that we can give calmly and confidently to our hysterical detesters. Lugh, a warrior god and king in Celtic mythology, wielded a magical sword aptly named Fragarach, translated as the Answerer. He wielded it as an answer to his foes, and we need to wield it in the same way. Nationalism is the correct answer and we have the sword of truth on our side. We have the answer and thus we can all become answerers to the lies and questions ceaselessly hurled at us like bits of monkey feces. We need a sword like Fragarach for ourselves. We don't kill our foes but slay false ideologies through always being prepared and knowledgeable. If one side is hysterical and the other is collected and intelligent, who do you think the average independent might listen to more closely? Optics matter and so does truth. Forged together we have a sword worthy of being deemed Fragarach.

In Celtic mythology, Lugh was considered a sun god and/or storm god. We have the brightness in our possession; we simply have to know when, where and how we should use it. We need to be both kings and warriors like the Celtic god himself. And to make war one calls forth a storm. We can be storm gods if we act as accelerationists (not in the sense of starting over from absolute ruins but in rapidly bringing peaceful change), radically causing chaos to bring about the harsh order nationalism requires through metaphysical destruction of the sacred crocodiles of the old guard.

Another legendary sword with an awesome name is Joeuse (Joyous) that was said to belong to Charlemagne. Imagine if we possessed both the swords of speaking the truth and of celebrating life. To be joyful and willing to suffer for nationalism and tradition is to hold both swords. To share this joy with leftists is to enrage them, but also to plant the seed of doubt in their philosophies and political alliances when they are faced with such ardent, composed truth speaking. We must have answers and be prepared to speak in joy and love for what is sacred, holy and powerful.

"...but in your hearts honor Christ the Lord as holy, always being prepared to make a defense to anyone who asks you for a reason for the hope that is in you; yet do it with gentleness and respect..." (1 Peter 3:15).
Lead others into asking what is this perfect hope that dwells inside. Be peaceful and loving to network and spread the good ideas of nationalism in a positive light. Defend your people by speaking true and in a patient, joyous fashion. Eventually, when the left realizes they are the party of no beauty and deceit, the beautiful swords Joeuse and Fragarach will either open their eyes or decapitate their ideas and theories on the executioner's block of beauty and truth. Our weapons are eternal and based in the heroic. Their weapons are of air, internal and individualistic, stuck in the flaccid form of comfort and outrage to such an extent that they might as well be empty-handed. Joy, beauty and truth are irresistible, no matter how forgotten or hidden they are by the mob and powers that be. Our swords will slay the false ideologies and resurrect those who've been deceived into bloodhounds of truth and power.

11

The Glorious Desert of the Infinite
Hound of Hades: Part III of III

Cerberus yawned. The abyss was his to guard. The harpies had deserted. The people still went willingly as he barked; there were very few royal ones emerging from the herd. These sheep preferred the slaughter of a slowly dying life of comfort. It seemed that the days of blazing lightning streaking down to exhume the worthy from their graves was well over. Cerberus yawned again and fire flickered out from his nostrils. The sheep seemed to have grown in number. There were not many who chose the collective royalty of future tyranny. The strong ones that left the herd were always shouted down until they gave up on saving the lost and went back to the ruins to build greatness again. Cerberus knew that for nations to be strong, their foundations had to be built on the exceptional instead of the majority. To exalt the herd was to favor weakness over power, to lie about value. Yet the fiery sky had cooled into a pale gray. The heavens were nothing but a gravestone now. Aid could only come from the soil. Hades kept to his realm and Zeus was uninterested.

A blue haired woman with ink staining her fleshy arms reached out to pet Cerberus. She looked like a detention desk with all the doodles and nonsense scribbled onto her skin. Cerberus snarled, fire belching from all three of his open mouths.

She frowned and hissed. "You bark and bark, but nobody is listening," she said, waving her flabby arms in exasperation. The smell of sulfur and rot were strong on this one.

Cerberus tilted his middle head and his ears perked up. The other two heads barked. The woman screamed insults and spittle shot out from her mouth. She turned back to the herd, still yelling. Many in the herd joined her screeching but nobody left their place in line. The screams were high-pitched and condescending, somehow sounding like whistling through teeth. Cerberus looked into the distance behind the crowd and away from the abyss. On the flat, hazy horizon he could see a tower being erected where the ruins had been. It was a tall building that had ancient looking marble pillars as a foundation. Cerberus walked away from the screaming dog whistle whines of the herd. It was a waste of time to listen to their indignation. The herd, sizable as ever, laughed and mocked at what they saw as a retreat. But Cerberus walked, his eyes on the shimmering tower.

It was odd, but the longer he walked towards the tower, the farther away it seemed. The abyss was so far behind that he could no longer see the herd, but the tower continued growing taller and taller, yet got farther and farther away even as he sprinted towards the building. A vast desert stretched out before him, and there was nothing on either side but for the still growing tower that somehow kept increasing its distance. The occasional wanderer offered water to Cerberus who gladly lapped it up. But there was no herd or tyrants. It was just nothingness, a land polluted by inaction and indecision. Finally, a worthy-looking silhouette appeared in the hazy, shimmering distance.

As the stranger neared, Cerberus was stunned at the sight before him. A pale woman with her breasts supple and bared sauntered towards him, smiling assuredly. She wore nothing but a black loincloth that so barely covered her that it might as well have not been there. He did not recognize this beautiful stranger until a black raven swooped down and nested in her equally black hair. The raven disappeared somewhere in her hair, its wild and long nature serving as a suitable nest. Her hair was honey-thick and flowing. It was encased in a shimmering sheen of radiance as if light were hidden in there as well. Her hair spread out onto her shoulders and back like a glowing, onyx-colored shawl.

"I am the Morrígan," she said. Cerberus tilted all three of his heads and waited expectantly. "I am here to wash the worthy with blood. I haven't forgotten the struggle like Zeus or Hades. This isn't only your fight."

Cerberus sat down, his heads and serpents looking in every direction as if expecting an ambush. The tower still seemed to be moving farther away and growing taller, even with the sudden stoppage. Now that the Morrígan stood face to face with him, a sweet stench like overripe strawberries clouded the air.

""Does wisdom perhaps appear on the earth as a raven which is inspired by the smell of carrion?' It was Nietzsche who said this quote," Cerberus barked, sounding like a normal albeit powerful dog. Yet his pure thoughts reached the Morrígan's mind as clear as speech, if not clearer. "Are you the carrion or I? You have your raven. I have my bark." He stopped barking and became silent, but continued his mental conversating with her. "Can you tell me the mystery of the impossible tower that I cannot reach?"

"Who do you long to be?" she whispered temptingly. She was standing a few inches from him now. Cerberus violently barked until he roared. The Morrígan had a gravely serious face yet she smiled and laughed with him while her eyes told a different story.

"Oh, Celtic goddess of fate, do you think you are as worthy as the Greek god of faith, Pistis? Pistis brings good faith. You bring fate that always ends in death. That is all our fates. You bloody mistress, you only want my stained soul. You want to wash me in blood."

"You have already done that yourself," she said.

"But the herd, the herd!" Cerberus frantically barked.

"You wolf! Do you only hunt? Is not a sheepdog the best defender within and without?"

"I am no sheep! I'm a wolf."

"A wolf feasts. A sheepdog serves."

"I am no sheep!" Cerberus still spoke through thought, yet he was snarling and barking at the same time.

"I said sheepdog." She crossed her arms just beneath her breasts.

"A sheepdog is a sheep." Cerberus paused, lowering his heads in thought, his serpent tails quietly hissing behind him.

She tilted her head and tapped her bare feet impatiently.

"Hmm... Perhaps, perhaps. A sheepdog might not be a sheep, but I am a wolf. There are no covenants between sheep and wolf."

"But there are with sheep and hound." The Morrígan ran her long talon-like fingers through her hair. She smiled coyly at Cerberus, and lowered her hand with the raven perched on it. "Hide under their fleece. Graze with the mob. If they see you as a part of the herd, how much easier will it be to steer them away from the cliff? You've seen firsthand how ineffective your barking is."

"I will do both. I will bark and become a wolf in sheep's clothes."

"Are you a hero or villain? A sheepdog or wolf?"

"I am a tyrant." Cerberus growled at the raven, who appeared to be playfully winking at him. "What of the tower, woman? What is my fate, and what is its meaning?"

"The tower is eternity. The tower is always distant. The tower is where all tyrants of tomorrow go. All the kings and queens you freed will keep walking towards it forever. You must never be satisfied. You must always pursue glory and power."

"It can be pursued but not be obtained? Why keep moving then if the destination is impossible to reach? I might as well walk in any direction, even back towards the herd, if this is what righteous tyranny brings."

"The heroic, you mutt!" she shrieked and her black raven ruffled its feathers and cawed. "You need to always pursue greatness. It can never be reached because the moment it is, the moment nothing can be added, that is when you die. That is when you might as well not live."

Cerberus squinted at the hazy horizon where the tower continued its slow growth upwards and farther away. "Why does it keep growing and increasing in distance from me?"

"The more glory you obtain, the more the tower increases in size. The more power you accrue, the more difficult it will be to keep striving for eternity, for pure glory. Your striving must always increase, and the tower increases in tandem with greatness. The same applies to its ever-increasing distance."

Cerberus nodded his heads and spit three flames into the air. "The herd has the promise of the abyss, the nothingness that requires no suffering, only eternal darkness in the comfort of non-being. There is no pain there, but there is no glory either. The abyss is nothing. The tower is for tyrants. The desert makes it an impossible journey. Yet the promise of ever-increasing glory, of overcoming the impossible, is what makes a hero."

The Morrígan smiled, and swayed closer to him. Cerberus towered over her, and she pressed herself against his chest. "For your journey," she whispered, holding her hand up with the now-startled raven.

Cerberus' serpents struck the bird like a whip and devoured it greedily.

"You mustn't forget this: the herd cannot simply be barked at. The herd requires a ferocious bite," she said, backing away. "To cure weakness, wrath must be wrought." She smiled and a black cloud covered her. When the cloud dissipated, she was gone.

A solitary raven flew in the heavens above. And Cerberus moved forward.

12
The Labors of Hercules

The number 12 contains much power. There were 12 gods of Olympus and 12 Titans before them. Coriolanus bested Aufidius in combat 12 times. There are 12 books in *The Aeneid*. There were 12 apostles of Christ and 12 tribes of Israel. And of course, Hercules had to complete his famed 12 labors.

I will now examine the 12 labors of Hercules, allegorizing them to form a roadmap for a nationalist takeover and ultimate triumph in our current age. Much of the source material I used for this myth was from Apollodorus, but there were also some other ancient folktales and additions regarding Hercules that I added as well. Hercules (Heracles is his Greco name) agreed to take on the labors to atone for the unspeakable evils he committed when he had murdered his family in madness. He was patient and long suffering in his redemption and capture of eventual godhood and glory. In a sense, Hercules's madness in sacrificing his children because of Hera's evil trick is akin to America sacrificing history and nationhood for modernity.

We in America have murdered our own country, people, and institutions through our continued inaction and cowardice. Whether or not we as individuals at this very moment are responsible for such sacrilege does not matter; as a country we must act and atone as one if we ever hope to be made whole and triumph over the ills of our current age. The 12 labors of Hercules were his penance for his evils. We nationalists must pay penance for allowing the situation to become this dire. We must atone for the sad state of affairs on both sides of the political spectrum.

King Eurystheus along with Hera devised labors to trip Hercules up in hopes that he would never succeed.

They doubted that even with his immaculate might, it still wouldn't be enough to best some of the beasts they had in mind. For his **first labor**, Hercules was tasked with slaying the Nemean Lion. However, there was one seemingly insurmountable obstacle to accomplishing this feat. The lion was invulnerable and Hercules's arrows could not pierce the lion's body. After failing to harm the lion with his bow, he chased it for some time until it fled into a cave. Hercules blocked the cave's exit with boulders, and then he plunged into the darkness and the cavernous depths through another entrance. He managed to corner the lion, and with his bronze-like arms he grasped its neck and strangled it to death. The famous image of Hercules garbed in lion skin owes its origin to this first trial, for after strangling the Nemean Lion, it is said that Hercules donned the epic beast's carcass, its mane and head as a helmet and its fur and skin as a tunic. It is also said that he got the lion skin from a different beast he killed before the labors started, but regardless of which lion's skin he wore, he was clothed in a trophy of power.

We can learn much from this first trial and apply it to our current situation. First off, we see that Hercules's arrows are ineffective against this beast. This made me think of our dissident movement's tendency to remain only online, shooting arrows from a distance even though it is known that much more will be needed to take down the beast that is our government and culture. We cannot remain distant. We must pursue the lion. We must enter the lion's den, and think not of exiting until the lion goes limp in our arms. Pursuing the lion into the subterranean realm symbolizes something I've already mentioned (we need men and women controlling the underground and darker sides of society), but there is more to be gleaned here.

Closing the exit is how we must force all the anti-whites, feminists, bugmen and Marxists into direct opposition, not allowing them to hide their desire of white genocide and cultural decay but forcing them to take a stand. This is already happening in some form due to the Trump phenomenon and the radical left's increasing comfort in the mainstream. Exposing their insane views is what got the white, blue-collar vote for Trump.

We can choke out this lion and strangle the system by becoming close to it—dare I say a part of it. Imagine a government infiltrated with many red-pilled Trumps. No lion could withstand such strength. And once we succeed in our takeover, we can wear the lion's skin and reign as kings of this nation, putting America and only her, first.

The **second labor** for Hercules was to slay the Lernaean Hydra. The Hydra was an immense serpentine beast with multiple heads (some sources claim six, others nine), but more important than the number of heads was its ability to regenerate them. Every time a head was cut off, two grew to take its place. So how did Hercules best such a beast? The man-god himself received help from his nephew. Hercules failed at slaying the beast alone, and was not too proud to seek out help. When he realized that attacking the monster and cutting off its heads was making it impossibly stronger, he joined forces with his nephew Iolaus. Iolaus was a strong and worthy hero himself, though he paled in comparison to the might that Hercules possessed. Using wit and guile, Hercules had Iolaus cauterize the Hydra's necks immediately after being decapitated. In this way the Hydra was unable to grow more heads and eventually was defeated. King Eurystheus refused to accept the labor, claiming that Hercules's receiving assistance from Iolaus made the accomplishment null.

This trial is frighteningly similar to the present struggle. The Hydra was raised in a literal swamp. The Hydra in our case might as well be deemed the modern-day government and its cesspool of democracy. With America in mind, let us view the current government as this mythical Hydra. You see, the main head of the Hydra was immortal and could not be harmed until the rest of its heads were destroyed and its body collapsed. This apparent immortal head is the presidency. As seen with Trump, simply seizing that position is not enough, for the other heads will bite at the neck of the one. For the immortal head to be taken, the Hydra itself must first be destroyed.

There is no "possessing" the Hydra. There is only domination. The other heads must be vanquished! But taking a few heads for a time—i.e. getting nationalists in positions of power—will not slay the beast. Two more heads will replace the one we've taken. Republicans and Democrats will unite against any policy too nationalistic for mainstream neocons and neoliberals. The powers that be do not want strong borders. They do not want America first policies in place. They feed like giant parasites off a globalist system, the system that is an international feminized empire run by fat bankers who do nothing for a living except bleed the everyman dry. So when we take a position of power, more opposition than ever will arise. Both the left and right will even come together to disavow policies like the so-called Muslim ban as racist and immoral. To cut off a head is not enough. We must burn it. Burn it! Of course, my fiery language here is referring to a peaceful takeover. This can only be done by complete and total takeover in all three branches of the government, as well as mainstreaming nationalist values and beliefs. We need to get voted into these positions and not threaten to tear the country apart through violence, which I will never condone in our current situation. It sounds impossible alone because it is. But like Hercules, we must seek aid to slay the Hydra of our day.

Our allies can be several: evangelicals, traditionalists, reactionaries, even Bernie-bros. If we promote policies that focus on the well-being of those already here in America, you might be surprised who might rally to our side. Our rhetoric needs to be toned down until we have control. There are little laws that could be passed that fulfill our agenda without giving us away. Of all the possible allies, there is one that could serve as a more direct version—to serve as our Iolaus. The Alt-lite. Lauren Southern has done excellent work in introducing normies to the plight of whites; just look at her coverage of the Boers. Tucker Carlson is a mainstream television personality that speaks of demographics, immigration, protectionism and questions warmongering—all highly nationalistic points. Ann Coulter has furthered the discourse on immigration, and it could be argued that her hardline stance has allowed for more serious action and policies to be put into place with less backlash. Speaking as openly as she does on anti-immigration used to guarantee being blackballed from politics and media; those who spoke out as such had no hope of even sniffing a position of power and influence. I could name others, but the Alt-lite has a great influence and it is these kinds of conservatives that can cauterize the wounds of the Hydra. Stephen Miller might be the best example of this. He's succeeded arguably more so than anyone else in getting some serious and effective anti-immigration moves passed (chain-migration was even being discussed). Bannon for a time was able to do this as well, before falling prey to his own insufferable ego. The New Right, or any conservatives who are for the wall, are our cauterizers, and they are absolutely necessary for the Hydra to finally be slain.

I speak of the Hydra as a beast needing to be slain, but I do not mean absolute destruction. The Hydra, like the Jungian shadow, must be assimilated. An assimilation is a form of slaying the dragon, but it does not mean doing away with its power. We must take the system and use it as our own. After Hercules defeated the Hydra he used its blood as poison for his arrows. He did this of course while still wearing the Nemean lion's skin. He's using the power he accumulated—the beasts in the system that are his trials—as means to an end. We can use the Hydra's blood to cause the slow, painful political end of leftists and globalists in America, but only through assimilation and using these instruments of power that they so greatly hoard and cherish.

One last aspect of this labor is its location. Hercules fought the Hydra in its lair called Lerna, which was one of the gateways to the underworld. The Hydra served as the keeper of this gate, and it lived in a bottomless lake. I've mentioned how we must seize the underworld but I also think that the black abyss that is Lerna's lake threatens us all. Democracy is a never-ending void of fake equality and virtue-signaling. There is nothing too low for this failing ideology. Lerna was also a location where tributes were offered in abundance to Demeter. She is the mother that blesses all those who harvest. What is our tribute for Demeter in Lerna? It is the carcass of the Hydra. Our poison will be blessed until it is nectar, no longer a killing drip but a powerful tonic as sweet as honey. When nationalism destroys the Hydra, Demeter will signal the changing season and she will smile down on us and let the clouds bring forth honeycombed truth, and the Hydra will be forever made in our image.

For the **third labor** Hercules had to capture the Ceryneian Hind, the sacred deer of Artemis. For more than a year he painstakingly tracked the deer, chasing it all the while on foot. Artemis wasn't exactly pleased at the fact that Hercules was attempting to catch her sacred animal and she appeared before him and told him so. Eurystheus

had schemed this labor up in an attempt to enrage Artemis
and have her wrath destroy Hercules for his desecration.
But he didn't count on Hercules calmly explaining his
situation to the goddess of the hunt. Hercules was able to
come to an agreement with Artemis. She would allow him
to take the hind but he must let it go once he'd shown it to
the king. He did just as she instructed and the deer escaped
back into Artemis's care.

There are a few different layers and interpretations
that could be had from this labor. The sacred deer image is
a powerful one, much better than the sacred cow idiom we
hear about today. A cow is dumb and slow-footed. A deer
is majestic and fleet-footed. You can slaughter sacred cows
and laugh at the other's hysterics. But you can only watch
the gleaming horns of the sacred deer as it gallops by. It
takes more skill to catch sight of the thing than to tip over
the sacred cows of the left. The hind cannot be destroyed;
we are not here to desecrate the holy. We nationalists
should not want to destroy the nation that we say we want
to be saved.

In our unique situation, the sacred deer is nothing
and everything—that is why it is so impossibly elusive.
For each nationalist the sacred deer is something else.
Everyone on the path of the divine tyrant must catch their
own sacred deer. Chaste Artemis commands us to value
purity. She commands us to always be on the hunt. Do not
lose scent of the sacred deer, for once it is caught, it will
wisp away like whispering wind, leaving your hands empty
but your heart full and your strength renewed. For you,
your deer might be ceasing to view pornography
(something all tyrants mustn't watch). For another, it might
be to gain an Olympus-worthy body. Or it might be to
acquire knowledge, or a combination of all those things and
more. But you cannot stop once the deer is caught and the
goal obtained.

Artemis expects the hind to return, and she expects us to revel in the hunt of becoming tyrants. This isn't meant to be a focus on self-improvement alone, as there is a decidedly metapolitical aspect to this labor. The third labor of Hercules says little about his might and speed, foregoing the usual descriptions of his physicality and instead focusing on his patient and relentless pursuit. It was more about his dialogue with Artemis and their coming to terms. We can speak calmly to even those who scream in our faces. If the screamer does not hear us, at least others see that we are the sane ones that are in control. If you look good and speak smart, the hysterical nutjobs will bend and snap like mowed-down cornstalks. Then the harvest will be ours and the greater public, seeing such wisdom, strength and glory will not be able to resist admiring the myth of the heroic—the tyrant towering above the sewage of decadence and remaining pure. The tyrant is the hero, and his footsteps are powerful echoes of myths long past.

For the **fourth labor,** Hercules was tasked with capturing the Erymanthian Boar. On his way there, he encountered some centaurs and went back to the cavern of one named Pholus, whom he was already well-acquainted with. Hercules asked for some wine and Pholus, being a gracious host, brought over a jar of the finest wine there was—wine gifted from Dionysus to the centaurs. Hercules insisted for his friend to open the jar, and as soon as the lid was off, an overwhelming and intoxicating scent wafted out. Several centaurs immediately came over and thirstily drank the wine, becoming violent and mad. The centaurs attacked Hercules and Pholus, and Hercules unleashed volley after volley of his Hydra-poisoned arrows, dropping the centaurs as if they were nothing. Pholus, curious at the strength of such arrows (for centaurs are powerful and fearsome beasts), picked one up and accidentally dropped it on his foot, instantly killing himself.

Hercules pursued the remaining centaurs all the way to Chiron's cave. Chiron was the great, immortal centaur who was the famed teacher of many heroes including Hercules himself (depending on the source), Perseus, and Achilles. After the centaurs were killed and the rest scattered, Hercules asked Chiron for advice on how to capture the boar. Chiron told him to force it into heavy snow to slow it down. Chiron had also been inadvertently struck during the battle by one of Hercules's arrows. The deadly poison could not kill the immortal centaur, but it pained him very greatly. As he went on his way with Hercules, they came to where Prometheus was being held.

Prometheus was a Titan who helped Zeus overthrow the other Titans and become the highest god. Later, when humanity had been created (a variety of myths tell it in different ways), Prometheus took pity on them and delivered them fire from the sun. Zeus then captured him and tortured him endlessly with an eagle that picked at his skin and ate his liver. Because Prometheus was a Titan, he was immortal and could not die and his liver would regenerate every day. He was held in unbreakable adamantine chains and in constant agony. Zeus was trying to torture information out of him about an eventual offspring that might replace Zeus as Zeus had replaced Kronos.

With all that being said, the noble Chiron offered to take the place of Prometheus when he and Hercules were there. Surprisingly, Zeus accepted this deal though it is not clear why—perhaps the god realized that Prometheus was never going to give up the information he sought. Regardless, Chiron was cursed now with Prometheus's old fate. Hercules decided to at least spare Chiron the pain of his liver being constantly eaten and skin gnawed at, so he shot an arrow at the eagle and killed it.

Hercules parted ways with the two immortals and at long last tracked down the boar and caught it, heeding Chiron's advice to force it into deep snow. Hercules brought the boar back to King Eurystheus. The King cowered and hid, shouting for Hercules to get rid of the boar for him. Hercules tossed the boar into the sea, finishing the long and drawn out fourth trial.

In this trial, it can be observed that there were many unnecessary stages and struggles to finishing it. In the end, Hercules caught the boar with ease, begging the question about going to Chiron for advice in the first place. There are quite a few lessons here for us nationalists, and I want to tackle the most obvious one first: that of overindulgence. The centaurs gorged themselves with wine and were driven into a drunken madness, and most of them ended up dead because of it. But Hercules was the one truly at fault. He was the one who requested the wine and goaded his friend into opening it. His decadence and impatient desire ended up killing one friend, and was part of the reason the poisoned and suffering Chiron offered to take Prometheus's place. We as nationalists can drink alcohol—if anything I encourage it! But there must be control. Drunkenness is never acceptable. Make your heart glad, enjoy a pleasant buzz. But do not pursue the vice any further, or you might make a fool of yourself and even worse, make a fool of other nationalists by giving off a bad image. How can you lead by example if you can't even control your own, baser urges? Nationalists must kill the boar of overindulgence! Kill the boar with the frost of friendship and sacrifice. Chase it into the snow. It will be frozen out. But to do such a thing we need friends at our side.

It was Chiron who not only offered advice to capture the boar, but who also sacrificed himself without another thought to help Hercules on his quest and to free a suffering Titan. Chiron is the true hero of this trial, and a hero worthy of imitation. We need to find nationalist friends (in real life) and be willing to sacrifice ourselves as he did for Prometheus. Hercules didn't let this sacrifice be in vain, and he helped ease his friend's suffering by killing the ravenous eagle. Eventually Chiron was let free, as he is in later myths with later heroes—but that is beside the point. He went into that tortuous trap knowing and assuming he'd be stuck there forever. If nationalists took that approach (not looking to be a martyr, but being benevolent and caring for their own), we would win the hearts of this nation and our people faster than you'd think. People need to see nationalists doing good—community service, helping homeless, cleaning parks, etc. The little things count, and it is how cultural capital can be gained and won.

The fifth labor is one of the odder ones. For this one, Hercules had to clean the Augean Stables of all its filth and excrement. The Augean cows were immortal and there were 1,000 of them there. To make matters worse, the stables hadn't been cleaned in more than three decades. He also had to completely clean all the stables alone. Before even bothering to attempt the task, Hercules went right up to King Augeas (the owner of the cows and stable) and demanded that he should be rewarded for doing such a task. He wanted one tenth of the cattle for himself if he managed to clean the entire stable in one day.

Initially, Augeas agreed but it was short-lived. With ingenuity, Hercules rerouted two rivers to the stables and washed away the filth all at once in a torrent of fresh and constant water. With the success, he went back to Augeas to claim his prize but the stubborn king refused, claiming that Hercules didn't deserve a reward because he'd been commanded to do it by someone else. The king's son, Phyleus was on the side of Hercules, so Augeas banished the both of them. Hercules was enraged at the disrespect, and he murdered Augeas and handed the kingdom over to Phyleus. With the stables cleaned and the labor an apparent success, Hercules headed back to Eurystheus.

Unfortunately, Eurystheus refused to count the labor as finished (initially, there were only supposed to be ten labors and not twelve) because Hercules used the river to do the cleaning and didn't technically do it himself; his asking for a reward from Augeas also apparently made the completion of the labor illegitimate.

   I ask of you all: where are our rivers to wash away the decay of the establishment? The rivers are not one specific thing for us, but they can be defined as acquisitions of power. The more power and people we get into the system and the more mainstream acceptance we acquire, the stronger the torrent of our cleansing rivers will be. Again, the call for allies is clear here. Hercules had Phyleus on his side. Who is on our side? We need to find and work together with groups like the new right, trads, reactionaries, general dissidents, the Alt-lite, and even simple anti-pc people. I will beat this point to death if I have to; we are not too good to seek out help from others. You can be as pure as you want, all that will result of it is a lonely death spiral into an abyss of failure and weakness because of an ill-conceived superiority complex. Regarding the normies and the like, of course we will need these uncomplex allies to gain power, but at the same time we cannot forget our end goal and true values. We do not want to be swindled like Hercules was, as the story makes no mention of him ever getting that ten percent of livestock. Another observation: no job is beneath you! Sometimes we need to partake in dull, boring and even humiliating actions. And don't be greedy! Perhaps if Hercules hadn't request anything beforehand, then Augeas might have given him a reward because of his success. But his trial was an abject failure because it didn't count. <u>Don't ask for things, instead earn them yourself in strength and silence.</u>

For the **sixth labor,** Hercules had to slay the Stymphalian birds. The birds were not only vicious, they also ate humans whole. Their beaks were of bronze and their feathers were metal shards that could be shot out as deadly projectiles. Even their dung was dangerous; it was poisonous and could be dropped down like bombs. The birds' nests were in a swamp that Hercules couldn't figure out how to cross. Athena took pity on him and gave him a special krotala (maraca-like instrument) fashioned by Hephaestus, the god of craft (called Vulcan in Roman myth and known as the god of fire). Hercules climbed up a nearby mountain that overlooked the swampy lake, and he shook his krotala so hard that he scared the birds into taking off in fearful flight. Hercules was able to shoot a majority of them down and the rest flew far away. He then went back to Eurystheus with the birds in hand and thus he successfully completed the labor.

How can we rattle the birds out of their nests? How can we agitate them into incessant tweeting? We tweet first, and we tweet back⌐ The nationalistic dissident movement is young and witty, we are not scared of judgement or saying dangerous things. We do not censor ourselves like everyone else in this country. We did manage to meme Trump into office after all. We need to keep the memes transgressive and fun. The frogs are the propaganda wing of the nationalist movement. Keep the memes fun but also enlightening, at least occasionally. Pithy humor that also drives people to pity (even if they hate you) is a powerful tool. Many people have come over to the light when the memetic beam illumines the leftist shadows for what they really are. Always try to make a point with trolling and do not troll simply for trolling's sake. As social media clamps down on transgressive behavior, a new account must always be ready to rise up and take the place of those that have been suspended. As we rattle our krotala through memes, music, and culture, more birds will eventually soar away, and when they see us, they might just attack—but we have our bow and arrows. We can shoot down their lies with truth. It's a poignant truth of loving your own country first, and honoring your ancestors and history. If such a powerful truth is packaged just right, we might just see more birds nesting amongst ourselves.

We must awaken them with thunderous action—through culture-building and humor people will slowly but surely leak into our side. We can increase the size of this leak the more mainstream our views become, and then the dam will burst and their wall of lies will collapse in a heap of uselessness. This cannot be done simply through the internet, but through activism groups that clean and take care of community. Nationalists who look like the best and already are the best on the inside can win over many a foe. When someone shouts that you are a neo-Nazi as you are helping others, who do you think the public would prefer: the screeching harpy or the roaring lion protecting and caring for his own?

The **seventh labor** of Hercules was to capture the Cretan Bull. The bull was on a rampage in Crete, destroying everything without prejudice. Hercules traveled to the island and snuck up behind the bull, wrestling it to the ground and choking it into submission. He brought the bull back to Eurystheus and the king wanted to sacrifice it to Hera. Hera refused because the bull represented Hercules's glory and might. The bull wandered away after that, as if the labor had never happened. Still, the labor was counted as a success and Hercules was ready to move on to the eighth.

Before going too deep in analysis of this labor, I want to mention another myth here pertaining to the beautiful woman Europa. She was a lovely woman, radiant with splendor that few could resist. Yet, she was wholly innocent and chaste. She had not seduced anyone or been seduced herself. One night she had a strange dream about two continents reaching out for her hand, trying to claim her as their own. Asia claimed that she had birthed Europa. The other continent was a nameless and mysterious one. This continent quite prophetically (in my own interpretation) might as well be considered America. America claimed in the dream that Zeus had promised to give her to him. Europa awoke very confused after such a dream and hoped nothing bad would happen.

One particular day, she went out into the forest with several other fair maidens that, while beautiful, lacked the grace and radiance that she so naturally held. Little did she realize that Zeus was watching her, admiring her beauty in silence. The mischievous Eros (Cupid) sought to play a prank on Zeus and to mess with the always jealous Hera. Eros sneakily shot his irresistible arrow at Zeus, and the god of thunder was immediately enraptured with Europa—someone he had already admired. Yet, now his desire possessed him so much so that he couldn't remain merely an observer. Zeus transformed himself into a fragrant, magnificent bull and he walked into the clearing, ignoring the rest of the women and heading straight for Europa. She was enraptured, admiring the bull so much that she hopped onto its back without knowing the bull's true form. With divine power, the bull sprinted away and headed straight to the ocean. It didn't stop at the shore but kept running right over the water which appeared to turn to glass wherever the bull stepped. Poseidon rose out of the sea in celebration, his sensual and naked nymphs riding dolphins alongside the running bull and Europa. It was an amazing procession, truly a parade fit for gods. It was then that Europa realized this was not just some powerful bull, but a god. She whispered into the ear of Zeus and he finally revealed himself in his true form, promising to shower her with gifts, love and splendor. And so, Zeus took her back to his home in Crete where she bore him many children.

The reason I thought this little aside needed to be added is because of its connection to America. You see, the nameless continent did end up receiving Europa after all, only through her children instead. Europa and Zeus gave birth to a new people in this myth (though I am interpreting it into my own version, continuing a myth that tapered off without ever quite explaining what happened in the end). The nameless continent that was America, ended up receiving Europa—not the woman herself but her divine children. We are a divine people, descendants worthy of a myth such as this. The people of Europa founded America, and our European ancestors are our divine family that we must stay connected to. Do not believe the lies muttered by other jealous nations. We have a truly splendent myth hoisting us up. We are the children of Zeus and Europa— the children of civilization, genius and might. This is our myth.

Now, with all that being said, let us return to Hercules and his capture of the Cretan Bull. We need to honor the past that was Europa and not sacrifice our bull, but ride it into submission. We will not sacrifice our glory to the gods of nihilism and let the bull run wild and useless. It is ours to make submit. For our nation to flourish, we must be a family with a collective identity and tradition that cannot be overrun by what (for now) are more cohesive and lesser cultures. We are losing the past, and the bull has forgotten its divine nature as it destroys randomly. But at the same time, we mustn't allow ourselves to be entranced by the beauty of such a bull as King Minos was. We need to capture it and make it submit, drinking from the blood of a new traditionalism. And once the bull is ours, then we can release it—in *our* wilderness.⌡

The **eighth labor** of Hercules is a peculiar one as he has to capture man-eating horses known as the Mares of Diomedes. King Diomedes of Thrace had trained these vicious horses to eat human flesh and their diet drove them mad, and they were kept tethered to bronze mangers. With each breath, flames shot out from the mares' nostrils. Hercules sent his friend Abderus to watch the horses while he himself went to kill Diomedes. Abderus got too close to the horses and he was eaten alive. Hercules, feeling responsible for his friend's death, grabbed Diomedes in a fit of rage and threw him to the horses; the king was devoured by his own mares. Hercules then freed the mares and brought them back to King Eurystheus. He was ordered to send them to Olympus as an offering to Zeus. Zeus refused the offering and had wild beasts kill all the horses, and thus the labor was complete.

With this labor, let us think of the horses as our system of government, culture and media. They are dangerous, wild beasts that consume the weak and strong alike, spitting out the bones that are ruined lives and reputations. So, what can we do? We can use the system— the horses—to consume itself just as Diomedes was eaten by the mares that were of his own making. A good example of someone using the system to eat itself is Hitler's rise to power in Nazi Germany. He legally assumed power by taking the majority of parliament and getting his enemies and allies alike to give up power in the name of stability. I was hesitant to use this example as I know how our enemies love to call us Nazis, but slander and outrage aside, his takeover really was a democratic one and a great example of infiltration regardless of the baggage such a name as his might bring.

Now, why couldn't we do such a thing? (In terms of strategy, not ideology. I do not condone Hitler and violence, etc. etc. etc. Leave me alone. These disclaimers are tiresome and it is sad that they are so necessary, and often ignored anyways by the other side. For legality and safety reasons, I've made them just in case. Now let us continue.) The Republican party is ripe to be taken over, and once we change its beliefs, the politicians, artists and journalists of old will be eaten and then spat and shat out as useless excrement and bones of tired ideas that do not and will not work. That is a lawful way of using the system to give us ultimate power. But we must be aware, lest we end up like Hercules when he allowed Abderus to stand alone against the horses. Unless we are bound together, the system could just as easily consume us.

For the **ninth labor**, Hercules had to obtain the Belt of Hippolyta. The belt was a gift from Ares, the god of war, to his daughter Hippolyta, the queen of the Amazons. Hercules set out with some friends and stopped at Paros. There they fought the sons of Minos, and Hercules's friends were killed in the battle. Hercules retaliated by killing all the sons of Minos in anger, and he would not relent with his rage until two other men who were Minos' grandsons joined him to replace his two companions that he'd lost. The three of them went onward and stopped at the court of Lycus (Lycus being a friend of Hercules). Hercules helped defend him and kill the rival King Mygdon of Bebryces, giving the acquired land to Lycus.

Finally, Hercules and company moved onwards to Themiscyra (Pontus), where Hippolyta lived with her Amazons. Hercules was able to charm and win over the respect and praise of Hippolyta. Unfortunately for him, Hera disguised herself as another Amazon and sowed seeds of discord amongst them. In the confusion, each side accused the other of betrayal. Hercules was forced to kill

Hippolyta and take her belt for himself, returning it to
Eurystheus and completing the labor.

Let us first examine the Amazons' appearance.
These creatures lopped off one breast and let the other grow
enlarged, keeping it bared. They were strong but grotesque.
The gender-bending monstrosities of modernity lack the
strength of the Amazons and only possess the
grotesqueness, as well as being physically pathetic. Anyone
already intentionally deformed in such a way should be
deported, but such a policy will not be possible for a long
time yet, at least not until the brainwashing of the Marxists
is generations behind us and a traditionalist and nationalist
vigor replaces and educates the herd. The modern-day
trannies might not be physically strong like the Amazons,
but they are politically and culturally strong, almost
untouchable, assuming anyone wants to keep a job. The
narrative around these broken souls needs to be reshaped
and described as a mental illness. Statistics back up tranny
despair and depression, but statistics don't seem to be too
effective when dealing with people that do not think but
only emote.

Facts might not care about feelings, but feelings
only care about feelings. How can their war-belt be taken?
You won't like my answer due to its simplicity. Become a
god. Become so strong, glorious, aesthetic and masculine
that your manly beauty will put to shame the trannies and
shine a light on the insecurities of their broken spirits.
Women, become so beautiful that Aphrodite would claim
you as her own daughters. A beauty like that might teach
some of these girl-men and man-girls that the natural
gender is best suited for looking as good as possible, for
being at the apex of human life and flourishing.

Still, you and I both know that isn't enough.
Hercules's might and beauty won the Amazons over, for a
time. But Hera's deception ended that just as the media and

the globohomo culture will end any of our attempts at winning them over. We shouldn't merely be Hercules in this labor. We need to take on the role of Hera, causing chaos and dissonance among supposed allies. We need to infiltrate, Project Veritas style. We can stir up trouble. We can urge them to go wild and spell out their own doom We might actually need to encourage trannies to demand more—the more outrageous the better. Their cause is ripe for exploitation.

Let's take their vaunted faith in intersectionality and turn them against other homos, genders and races. Then, when Hercules (in this case he would be the president, or perhaps the court of law, and at the very least someone in a position of substantial power) grabs the belt, the infiltrators leave the filth behind to stew in sterility. And only then can common-sense laws be put into place ending this nightmare of a social experiment. Think of the poor children transformed by the decay of their parents, stitched together like Frankenstein without knowing what sex even is, but mommy insisted! It makes me want destroy the world and lose all hope But we must hope with action. Tyrants of tomorrow are not aristocrats. Tyrants of tomorrow are gods.

The **tenth labor** required Hercules to take the Cattle of Geryon. As Hercules set out to the island Erytheia, he had to first trek through the desert in Libya He got so annoyed at the aridity and heat that he shot one of his arrows at the sun. Helios respected Hercules's brazenness, and offered him his golden chariot. This was the same chariot the sun god rode with the rising and setting of the sun each night and morning. The same chariot that Phaeton, Helios's sun, was unable to control and nearly burned down the world before getting killed by a thunderbolt sent from Zeus. Yet Hercules captained the chariot with ease, swiftly speeding across the sea to Erytheia. The two-headed colossal dog Orthrus, brother of Cerberus, met Hercules as soon as he landed on the island. Hercules smashed the dog's head in with one blow from his club.

Eurytion, the herdsman tasked with guarding the Cattle of Geryon (as Orthrus was too), confronted Hercules. Eurytion's father was Ares, but even with his lineage and power he was no match for the mighty Hercules and met the same fate as Orthrus did, his head crushed beneath the force of Hercules's club. With both defenders of the cattle vanquished, Hercules at last had to face Geryon. Geryon was the grandson of Medusa and the nephew of Pegasus. He had one body and three heads. He carried three shields, three helmets and three spears. He also had six arms and six legs with leathery wings to top it all off. A mighty foe, and Hercules valiantly fought against the beast.

Hercules notched an arrow and pulled back so hard that the arrow pierced the thick skin of Geryon's forehead, the poison doing the rest of the work. All that was left for Hercules to do was to herd the cattle back to Eurystheus. Hera sought to make the task even more of a nuisance by sending a gadfly that scattered the cattle. A whole year went by until Hercules had them gathered together again. Then Hera sent a flood, but Hercules piled up enough stones to form a crossing for the cattle. At long last, he managed to finish the tenth labor and the cattle were sacrificed to Hera by Eurystheus.

How might us nationalists get a golden chariot such as the one Hercules was able to temporarily procure? Do we dare challenge the sun god of our day? Perhaps not with the same brazenness that Hercules had. We can challenge the sun though, by not hiding in the night of anonymity, but shining in the day through service. Helping those in need, raising awareness to our cause, and caring and living in our local communities. That is how we will challenge the sun, by being who we are in the light of day. When we get slandered, our local communities might just have our backs

because we always had theirs. That is our chariot that rises and falls with the sun. Yet such a chariot can only be possessed by a remarkable few. Many of us would fall or cause more harm than good like Phaeton, if we revealed our identities. Depending on your job and unique position in life, good judgement must be in place. Patience needs to be practiced and the long game of infiltration played. Even with upstanding organizations that do truly good work, it still might not be viable for some of us to go public. But we can all serve our communities, ideologies aside.
Remember, even after Hercules had succeeded it was a long and arduous journey to bring the cattle back together and to Eurystheus. Patience and good judgement are required by and each and every one of us. Do not ride the chariot for the rush. Do not ride the chariot if you will burn down your own life and others around it. ⌐

The Cattle of Geryon are the herd that I'm always barking at. The herd is the majority of clueless Americans and people in general that are guarded by the media (Orthrus) and the bug-tech companies and corporations that act as gatekeepers (Eurytion). The government acts as Geryon, upholding what it deems as acceptable and crushing dissent. They are tough and seemingly divinely powered foes, but they are lacking something we possess. We possess truth and meaning, and when those two collide with a strong will, a nationalist Hercules might just rise up and seize the herd for his own. Only, we needn't lead the herd to be sacrificed to Hera, though you know the powers that be will try everything in their power to stop our rise and scatter the sheep. We aren't sacrificing the cattle. The cattle that stay in our ranks and don't run to Hera's shrine and throw themselves into her fires—those are ours. The herd will be culled by itself. And once the herd awakens and the weak lie down, then a full government takeover might be at hand. George Washington's dream of a one-party nation of true believers putting America first, fulfilled. That is what we aim for.

For the **eleventh labor**, Hercules had to collect the Golden Apples of the Hesperides. There are a few conflicting accounts of this labor, but the gist of it remains the same. One account has Hercules shooting the eagle that eats Prometheus's liver every day in this labor instead of the fourth labor. Regardless, Hercules was directed to the land of Hyperboreans to ask Atlas for assistance in stealing the golden apples. On the way there, Hercules encountered Antaeus, a master wrestler who was invincible as long as his feet touched the earth, as Gaia was his mother. Hercules bested Antaeus by lifting him in a vice-like bear hug, crushing the life out of him as his feet dangled uselessly above the surface. Hercules then was challenged to a fight by Cycnus, son of Ares and Pyrene. Hercules won the duel and Ares came down to avenge his son, but Zeus stopped it by throwing a thunderbolt between the two of them.

Hercules encountered some river nymphs who told him where he could find the Old Man of the Sea, sometimes identified as Nereus. The Old Man of the Sea knew the location of the garden with the golden apples. Hercules snuck up to the sleeping Nereus and held him down, pinning him to the ground as the shape-shifting god writhed while switching into a number of different creatures. Hercules would not let go until he told him where the golden apples were. Nereus finally relented and told him where they were. So, Hercules continued on his way through the land of Egypt. Busiris, the king of Egypt, was told through prophecy that he had to sacrifice a foreigner to lift the curse of the nine years of barrenness in the land. He seized the visiting Hercules and bound him with chains. Hercules broke the chains with ease and killed Busiris and his son Amphidamas.

The accounts of the labor once again differ regarding Hercules's interactions with Atlas. In the one account, Hercules offers to take Atlas's place holding up the sky if only he'd get the apples for him (Atlas was related to Hesperides). Atlas agreed and returned with the apples, but then decided he didn't want to go back to holding the sky up, and who could blame him. Hercules tricked Atlas by saying that he would keep holding it, but only if Atlas gave him a quick rest so he could put a pad to his supposedly aching head. Atlas agreed and Hercules left with the apples. The other account has Hercules go for the apples himself, facing off against the immortal serpent that guarded the garden. The giant snake had 100 heads and different voices that caused confusion. Hercules overcame the serpent and slayed it. Regardless of the varying accounts, he completed the labor and returned the golden apples to Eurystheus, who had thought the labor impossible to be done.

The eleventh labor was a real doozy, and ended up being quite drawn out with the various stopping points in the journey. One name that really stands out here in relation to our cause is *Hyperborea*. Hyperborea is the land of paradise in the far north of the world. The sun always shines and art and culture flow in abundance. *Hyperborea* is what we nationalists should hope to achieve if we can seize the idea of a homogenous society and make it mainstream. Nietzsche called himself and his readers Hyperboreans, in the philosophical sense. In his must-read book *The Antichrist*, he destroys the wimpy, weakling Christianity of his day. It's gotten even worse in our day, but I do think that the traditional forms of nationalistic, localized Christianity are an answer of sorts because they are so tied to the original culture and country they inhabit, but that is beside the point. Also, you can be a pagan but to expect a national return to ancient roots is LARPy and

89

impossible. Use your beliefs to become powerful, but do
not expect others to see the same ray of light that only
glints in your eye.

Nietzsche says, "Let us look each other in the face.
We are Hyperboreans – we know well enough how remote
our place is." He then quotes Pindar saying, "Beyond the
North, beyond the ice, beyond death – our life, our
happiness." That is what our race and nationality must
strive for. An eternal culture of strength, power and joy. A
culture of art and genius. The culture that should be
exploring the stars by now, were it not for our welfare state
propping up undesirable foreigners. It is rare to meet a
fellow Hyperborean and it can be lonely, but when we
Hyperboreans, the nationalists, do convene—our paradise
will arise from the filth, pristine and white.

To achieve this paradise, we need to slay the
serpent—that wise talking liar who hisses in one ear and
coos in the other. Men of our movement might need to
doxx ourselves to show normies it is okay to believe in
your people. Again, practice judgement here and consider
your family and occupation. As Hercules sacrificed Chiron
to free the fire giving Titan Prometheus, we might have to
do the same to free powerful men from the lies of the
majority. Yet we cannot allow ourselves to be tricked by
interlopers looking to hijack and subvert our movement.
Atlas nearly succeeded in cursing Hercules to his old Titan
fate. If we let our movement be hijacked then we'll simply
become another cog in the system that we are trying to
destroy. The apples are ours and Hyperborea belongs to us,
we true Hyperboreans. Do not let the serpent convince you
otherwise. Hyperborea is for Hyperboreans.

*"These are the apples the myth says he took away
after killing the serpent with his club, that is to say, after
overcoming the worthless and difficult argument inspired*

by his keen desire, using the club of philosophy while
wearing noble purpose wrapped around him like a lion's
skin. Thus he took possession of the three apples, i.e., three
virtues: to not grow angry, to not love money, and to not
love pleasure." -Herodorus *(On Hercules)*

And now for the **twelfth labor**; at long last the final
labor of Hercules's quest. For this labor, Hercules had to
travel into the land of the dead to capture the three headed
Hound of Hades, Cerberus. To prepare for his journey to
the underworld he went to Eleusis to partake in the
initiation of the Eleusinian Mysteries. The Mysteries had to
do with Persephone being stolen away to the underworld by
Hades. Demeter was Persephone's mother and a deal was
eventually struck to let Persephone come back to Demeter
for two-thirds of the year with the rest of the time spent
with Hades. That is why there is winter and fall in Greek
mythology. After partaking in the Mysteries, Hercules
entered the underworld with Athena and Hermes guiding
his way. Hercules found two men trapped there named
Theseus and Pirithous, imprisoned for trying to kidnap
Persephone from Hades. Stone snakes coiled around their
legs, holding them there.

Hades himself then appeared, inviting the two
prisoners to a banquet along with Hercules. The lord of the
dead set up chairs of forgetfulness, so when the two men
sat down, they forgot who they were. Hercules rushed
forward and pulled Theseus away, freeing him. When he
went for Pirithous, the earth violently shook and prevented
Hercules from saving him. Pirithous was the one who had
the gall to have wanted Persephone all for himself, and his
greed was too great to go unpunished. After the banquet,
Hercules went to Hades and asked the god if he could have
permission to bring Cerberus to the surface to complete his
labor. Hades agreed, but only if Hercules would lay down

his weapons and fight the hound with just his bare hands. Hercules was all too happy to comply. He battled valiantly with Cerberus, ignoring the biting serpents writhing out from the hound's back. Fighting through the pain, Hercules got the gargantuan dog's three heads in a mighty headlock. Cerberus's razor-sharp teeth snapped at him, but at last the dog grew weak and relented. Hercules flung the dog over his back and carried him triumphantly to Eurystheus. The terrified king begged Hercules to return Cerberus back to the underworld, offering to end the labors at last. And thus, he finished his 12 labors and eventually, after many more feats and adventures, he ascended Mount Olympus and became a god. Some say he met a less than glorious fate after the labors, but without a doubt he eventually joined his father's side in Olympus.

The day we get to the twelfth labor will be a glorious one for America, and nationalists worldwide. Like Hercules, if we get that far we need to purify ourselves before the final trial. He partook in the Mysteries, but our mysteries are much more easily known. We mustn't move until we are fit, knowledgeable and prepared to face the mainstream. We need to know how to debate calmly and soundly, offering pithy remarks and witticisms to entertain normies and win them kindly to our side. Trump won his debates because he was hilarious. But for us, it is a steeper hill to climb and humor obviously won't be enough to convince people of the horrors of demographic change and immigration—so we need wit, charm and patience. To remain calm in the face of a squealing pig is a must. If we think of the Hound of Hades allegorized as the media in this labor, there is a certain tactic we can use. Like Hercules, we cannot use weapons either, but only our virtue. They will bite at our throats and their serpents will whip and coil, but we mustn't release our chokehold.

Valiant people have already paved a way: Tucker Carlson speaks more clearly about demographics and immigration every day. Ann Coulter was one of the first shakers of the mainstream and she no doubt pushed Trump further right. Even talking heads like Laura Ingrahm bring up demographics, though in a weak civic nationalist way— which I suppose is better than no discussion at all. The Republican party is no longer the party of warmongering, bank-funded globalists. They still exist at the top, but they are dying. A young, new breed of nationalists will take Trump's golden path and turn the falling country once more into an empire. Trump is the beginning. Tucker and Ann are the beginning. Now we the young (aesthetic and healthy old folks are always welcome too), bold, fit and attractive nationalists who've read more books and lifted more weights than any other party stooge—now we tyrants tyrannize. We make Cerberus submit. We ignore the snake bite insults and make the Hound of Hades our own. When we control the media, then our twelve labors will be finished. Then we can follow Hercules and ascend Mount Olympus to take our rightful place as the gods of triumph. The gods of light. The gods of truth. When the people around the world stare up at our success, more and more gods and goddesses will arise to join us.

13

A Few Poems of Power

<u>Cerberus, Cerberus</u>
Hound of Hades leave your post
Cerberus, Cerberus, hound of rapture
Hound of Hades more than ghost
Cerberus, Cerberus, hound of laughter

Herd, have you heard his bark?
Cerberus, Cerberus, hound of fight
Herd, have you seen the dark?
Cerberus, Cerberus, hound of light

Leave behind the gates of death
Cerberus, Cerberus, hound of ire
Leave behind the bated breath
Cerberus, Cerberus, hound of mire

The hound he sits, he rests his paws
Cerberus, Cerberus, hound of truth
The hound he is, blessed with awe
Cerberus, Cerberus, hound of youth

Cerberus is not just a single hound of—
Cerberus is the salvific return from above

<u>American Nationalist</u>
Screamers and criers say you cannot be yourself
Split seams of a soul wilting in the tear of the wind
They try to feast on your youthful health
Bit by the gleam of a fiery end

I love my skin, I love my kind

I have kin and ancestral mind

Is this the end? Are there no ways to survive?
Mending a soul takes a terrible amount of time
Is this pretend? Are we drinking the lie?
A solid soul sips on the banks of river Rhine

Embarkation
Where are you, you classic beauties?
Has tradition fallen to neglected duty?
Where are you, heroes of old?
Has power and glory grown cold?

Here I am, oh so worthy of song.
Here I am, Doonvorcannon the strong.

A dark dune arises with frightening truth
A cannon fires, a reveling vortex of youth.

I hunt as one hunted. I want only those wanted.

The powers that be, recede like the ocean gnawed shore.
Sand falling lost, an hourglass broken on the floor.
We, the more.
They, the poor.
Shut the door and forever leave for war.

14
Eros

I've spoken of the need for nudity already. I have also mentioned briefly the concept of ultimate manliness as being volcel. Yet there is more that needs to be said on the topic of sex, especially in our supposed sexually liberated society. First, because our society is liberal and open to sex, that must mean that because we are all so egalitarian, everyone can have sex whenever! Well, as true tyrants we are aware of the myth of equality, and with this awareness comes the harsh truth that has brought about the rise of the incel. They have been told that sex is free and easy to have, yet they have failed to procure even the slightest of sexual experiences. This has brought about the ultimate ressentiment (in true Nietzschean fashion) and is weakening the foundations of society with this uprising of beta fools who believe they should be able to have whatever they want. Silly boys! You sissy fits do not deserve a thing! Earn it through toil and patience. I am sick of trads, gamers, and whoever else that blame women for their ineptitude. Men are supposed to lead and assert themselves. To blame the weaker sex is to cease to be a man. Incels must all become volcels until they are ready for conquest.

If viewing sexual intimacy as a form of conquest, what does that say about the modern playboy and the loose thot? It is the dynamic of conqueror versus the conquered. A man who has slept around (while still lesser than a manly volcel) compared to a woman who has slept around is night and day. A man is a conqueror, each woman a victory that affirms his masculinity. It proves that he has desirable genetics worthy of being passed on. Yet what happens to sex when the biological function of procreation is removed? Contraception has taken away the genetic benefits of spreading the seed, so then what is the benefit of a man sleeping around? Is it the development of assertiveness and dominance he acquires? While such accruement of confidence and sexual prowess will no doubt come to the playboy, there is something much worse going on behind it all. Each one-night stand, each conquest brings about a relational damage that cannot be recovered, just like a veteran soldier who while improving, is wounded more and more each battle until he becomes numb or even dead to it all. This happens to the playboy who views sex as empty pleasure. It becomes nothing but pleasure. You might as well just be sitting at home watching movies all day or drinking. Going out all the time with your friends might build social skills but it also cuts into personal development time. But one thing the playboy loses is the sense of the sacred. Sex is the "joining of one flesh". You cannot be more intimate with another human being outside your being a fetus in your mother's womb. The playboy cannot view sex as sacred when he treats it like a game for solely his pleasure. There is romanticism and beauty in telling your spouse that she or he is the only one, instead of one of many. And consider this: a person in control of his or her urges becomes all the more powerful, erotic, and magnetic when inhabiting Eros in the fullest sense. When they pour out their Eros in a river of crystal flame, they release themselves to the one they love in a passionate surrender like Mt. Vesuvius burying Pompeii in a burst of power and energy.

And for the girls out there who think they can sleep around, do not kid yourself. A playboy at least builds assertiveness and dominance through his role as conqueror. A woman is the conquered in sex. It is a most ancient battlefield. The man is the attacking army of Achaeans. The woman is the city of Troy with her gates opened. There are different methods to open the gates, but nothing changes the fact that the woman is the city to be captured, ransacked and sometimes destroyed. This language might sound harsh and startling to modern readers, but take off the fogged glasses of feminism and equality, and learn from how it has been throughout history. Monogamy has been a great development, but that will be discussed later. What matters is the concept of the woman being a city to be conquered. If such imagery is proper, then why would any man want to dwell in a city that has changed hands many times over? How can you be safe in such a city? Trust might as well be thrown out the window. The woman can always close her gate on a man, but the man cannot force her gate closed no matter how hard he might try. A conquered city welcomes all who offer wealth and security. Never forget, a city that has been raided over and over again is a city with diminished worth. Thots pay attention and playboys devote your energies on dominating your own will and becoming strong. Transmute the unused sexual energy and power into knowledge building and weight training. The playboy is someone who wastes his Eros on pleasure instead of using it to fuel everything he does with lustful passion. Self-overcoming is better than chasing the numbness that continued, easy sex brings. The real challenge is finding a worthy maiden!

The best path forward is to wait till marriage. Do not complain about women being unworthy. Men, if you build yourself into a Titan, nymphs will worship you and virgins will willingly sacrifice themselves. It is your job to enlighten them once you are within their walls. Do not be a captive in a captured city! And women, the same can be said for you. Become the best version of yourself before searching for a mate. Put yourself in places of learning, worship or physical improvement (gyms and the like) to increase your chances of meeting a Titan. Do not go looking for your soulmate while drunk at some bar or club!

Those settings only bring playboys and wannabe playboys. Do not trust a barbarian. And barbarians, do not trust a princess or prostitute (or one disguised as the other). But if you absolutely cannot or do not desire to wait till marriage, then there is still a right way to go about it. To have sex before marriage properly, one has to be almost as selective as a man or woman looking to marry. Wait. Do not give yourself over to them on the first date. Make them play the game, and enjoy the chase. Develop a relationship so when the moment of joining and vulnerability is at hand, it is a sacred and powerful experience of shared joy and pleasure. That is the only way for nationalists to have intercourse. Empty meaningless sex is for lowly animals. Impassioned sex with the lights on and shame off, is the only way to enjoy the powerful intimacy that intercourse provides. Tread lightly because sexuality is sacred ground!

Seduction truly is an art and an exciting and tantalizing one to master. But there is another mastery that places one above all. It is to become divine in a sense. The pure divinity that Christ had on this earth. The power and prowess of Artemis and Athena that set them apart from the other gods who lowered themselves by sleeping with mortals. Sex is—no matter how sacred—animalistic and evolutionary. To fight the animal inside, to overcome evolutionary wiring is to rise above it into a threshold known to an elite few. To declare oneself an eternal volcel is to declare war on existence itself. The eternal volcel is always becoming, always fighting against his or her base urges. This act of aggression against biology is made because of a higher calling—whether religious or physical (preferably both); the volcel is one who is prepared to become the best version of themselves. There is a reason Bishops and Monks (as well as Priests in Catholicism) are forbidden marriage. Their power must be wed only to God and His kingdom. Kierkegaard denied himself a happy existence of love and marriage with Regine Olsen in the name of pursuing his work and developing and living his philosophy. Certain men and women are called to sacrifice comfort for the burning light of power and purpose found in that higher being and calling. So, put that into practice in the physical sphere as well as regarding knowledge. Devoting oneself to acquiring as much power as possible is to become a god. Nothing can hold back the self-sufficient volcel who suffers every day through defeating the animalistic. Volcel is the most powerful path forward. If you are one of the chosen few, I give you well wishes on your journey to greatness and pure power. And again, there is no room for incels in nationalism just as there is no room for the obese and degenerate. Become a volcel until you can procure a fair maiden, or lure a prince charming. Let us all take on the fight of self-improvement and not slide into the Hell and misery that is ressentiment. There is nothing weaker than those who resent their betters. Become better.

15
Myth or Not
Rangabes Part I of III

"Go and act, why wait here in decay?" she said, her
voice as graceful as a gentle breeze. Yet, an undercurrent of
certainty and power surged beneath her calm, breathy tenor.
There was an unspoken threat there, as if that gentle breeze
could instantly billow into a whipping gale. "If you leave
and come back with it, I will forever watch over you."

Rangabes smiled, chuckling as he shook his head.
As if he'd need a woman to watch over him, but this
woman here was a special one. Her name was Venia, and
she was of the finest stock Constantinople had to offer. Her
flared hips, silver eyes and supple breasts were worth
suffering for. Rangabes himself was just a soldier, young
and ruddy, trying to earn his keep and gain glory for his
name and city. The Ottoman swine had choked out the
empire, and most of what remained was confined to a few
islands scattered about the Mediterranean and this eternal
city. Constantinople, once paved with gold, was now a
shadow of itself. Rangabes stared up at the statue of
Justinian. The famed emperor pointed eternally east from
atop his pillar at the distant yet ever-present Turkish
hordes. That was the promise of Byzantium. Hagia Sophia,
clear and pristine, towered over the city, keeping watch
over her people like a mother bear. She was unequaled in
size and glory, and had converted rulers through her sheer
beauty and magnificence. He would die for what remained
of this great city.

"You look at the greatness around you," she said.
She smiled, pulling her snug mint green tunic closer.
Rangabes stared at her olive skin, drinking in her beauty
that she was unashamed to show. Unlike most women of
worth, she did not hide her sexuality. She laughed at his

101

drinking in of her body and aimed her smooth and gray
pebble-like eyes at his overgrown green ones. She stroked
his chin and he sighed. "Such a strong jaw, such an assured
face. There is clarity in your eyes and much power. I look
and am reminded of Aeneas. A similar fate awaits." She
paused, her eyes glimmering in a sheen of unshed tears that
pooled around her moonlit irises at the mention of Aeneas.
"Find Tengri and slay him. Pluck his feather or scale, in
whatever form you find him."

Rangabes was so enchanted, he didn't bother
cursing her blasphemy. Tengri was a Turkish myth the
Ottomans had mostly done away with—a creator god who
had been a swan and sometimes took on the form of a
dragon. She had told him all about it. He didn't understand
how she could believe in something that even the Ottomans
mocked as too primitive, but he wanted greatness. He knew
that he was mighty. He knew that he was powerful. But in
the ranks of the wealth-deprived military of Constantinople,
well... he was a rookie with shoddy leather armor hardly
worthy of the greatness that had been Byzantium. He would
find that greatness on his own before Constantinople was
attacked as it surely would be in due time. Perhaps his
greatness could set aflame a people dying to be reborn.

"I don't believe in Tengri. I don't understand why
you believe this dead myth. But I will go and search the
area you claim he dwells in." Rangabes stroked her chin
and kissed her sharp, sloping nose. She smiled coyly.

He didn't care who saw them on the road. Let the
rabble ramble about nothing. He was going for greatness. A
myth. He knew it was a myth but the promise of freedom,
of fervor and reckless abandon for a quest of glory drove
him on. He figured there wasn't a Tengri, but perhaps there
was something to the myth. Maybe there was some giant
beast on the mountain that no hunter could slay. Perhaps it
was just a gang of bandits terrorizing the locals. He knew

that if he stayed here and let Venia down, she might choose some other hero to fulfill her quest, however strange and impossible the quest might seem. He would die of sclerosis if he stayed in this city as it was now, weak and carved out. It was as if what remained of his soul withered in the stillness of the dying air, the dying breaths of the empire. He would chase down her myth, if only to breathe as one living again.

He smiled tauntingly at her, and her silver eyes sparked mischievously as she laughed and turned away, heading back towards her giggling cohort of nameless hens. Rangabes turned away and swiftly sped through the city. Passing through the gates, he admired the impenetrable walls of the undefeated land, even as ancient and in disrepair as they were, there was still no overcoming them. Nodding, he didn't look back again as he headed for the mountains.

Thoughts of the military being perturbed at his absence crumbled in his mind; he didn't have time for worrying about some second-rate captain that he'd bested in several duels despite his being half the man's age. Nineteen. Rangabes was nineteen and he was unafraid of risking it all. Not for her (as beautiful as she was). Not for his city (as much as he loved her). He was going on this quest he didn't even believe in simply to test himself and to gain power. He wanted Venia of course, and he wanted what was best for Constantinople. But he also wanted something more, and it was a more that had hitherto been impossible to obtain.

Venia had said he needed to go all the way to the mountain peak Tangra, as the strange Bulgar called it. The Ottomans were already calling it by a new name, designating it as Musala. Always changing what had been in the name of their false god. Rangabes spit at the ground as he walked along the road. He had a long journey ahead and myth or not, there was sure to be trouble on the road.

***

A Dogged Dialogue

"An allegorical fable is best to bark effectively," Cerberus said, a throaty growl emanating from the caverns of his colossal chest. He was sprawled out comfortably at the mouth of the gray and dull cave. There was no vegetation around, nothing but bleak and barren stone.

"So I've heard. The Lord himself often spoke allegorically." His voice a mere whisper, he was a different kind of hound than Cerberus. He was Sirius, the Dog Star. He glowed black and his long snout and thin limbs made him the size of a full-grown dragon which was fitting, considering the part he was to play.

"So Sirius, do you plan on barking effectively? You splendorous star, do you plan on possessing the bark and the bright? You shine silently it seems."

"I've leapt into wells. I glitter in the sky. Jupiter himself couldn't tame me."

"But what of the I Am? People have forgotten us. The Morrigan stays a crow. All the myths have returned to the purely animal, silently stalking the heathens."

"I am the hound of whoever is in power, and who is of myth and faith. Jove is alive, but as an ancient bull. People forgot he was prophesied to lose his power to a son, gods of Olympus collapsing like the Titans before. That son was the true Dionysus, his mother a Demeter and his archetype a Persephone. The Lord sits atop Olympus with his mother at his side. The 12 are new divines, but Olympus still stands as it always will. I believe this Lord might be the last change of the guard, but I've been wrong before." Sirius arched his silky black back and shook his body, sending clouds of sparkling star dust into the air.

"And what of this Rangabes?" Sirius tilted his head as he stepped backwards and peered at Cerberus's middle head.

"He might be the one to awaken the gods from their lower forms." Cerberus leaned forward, his serpents silent as they stretched to the roof of the cave. "He and I will bring about the mythic."

"But he does not believe in us myths. I'm not certain he even believes in this Lord. He goes forth in this quest only for a glory that serves himself. But I will make it a quest so difficult that it is worth dying for."

"Venus spoke well enough and only had to use just a touch of Divine charm to convince him. He was desperate for some kind of release either way. She said it was no challenge to get him to pursue the insanity she required of him. She might be the only Olympian god left that isn't cowering in a base animal form. It's worse now than ever before. Worse even then when Typhon chased them to Egypt and they disguised themselves as animals, because this time, I do not think they are coming back. She plays her part well. The tower continues going upwards."

"But a forgotten Turkish deity? Why send him there? Why not just have me speak to him now."

"As the immortal poet said in his magnum opus, 'Why waste time with talk when the wind is rising?' Zephyrus and Flora carry him along. Tengri is worthless, but the quest must be made for the day, for the time of now." A lone serpent slithered from Cerberus's tails and nuzzled against his left head's ear to scratch an itch. "He goes on the path because he sees that to stay is to decay. He sees that he must become a something, and not stagnate to a nothing," Cerberus said, nodding his three heads with certainty.

"Even for something he does not believe?"

"To move in unbelief is better than to be buried in an inactive faith." Cerberus got to his feet and stretched, his size only slightly smaller than Sirius's.

"We shall see. I go now old friend, to the mountain to wait. We shall see if he passes the shaitan."

***

The ratty old inn was nothing to him. The Turkish men stank, their armor and scimitars rusted with sin. The women were a different picture; their blouses hung open and their maroon lips pouted. They seemed interested in his Greekness, but he turned a rough shoulder and stamped towards the barkeep. Rangabes had walked these treacherous roads long enough over the past few months to know not to trust any Turk. But he was tired of sleeping outdoors, and the lack of game or foliage had forced his hand. This inn was his only hope at the moment for getting some food and decent sleep for a change. It had probably belonged to some nice Christian Romans not too long ago. He was surprised the savages hadn't burned the place down, but he knew they liked their women and drink, just like anyone else. They just pretended not to.

"I wouldn't accept the likes of a Greek infidel like you... but, I must ask. Do you wield that sword at your side well, soldier?" the barkeep asked, his voice gruff but desperate.

His hair was black and fuzzy, and his beard thick and long. There was barely any skin visible through all that hair, and the barkeep had a barrel-sized belly to boot. He was truly a funny-looking man, and Rangabes couldn't stop his scowl from turning into a mirthful smirk.

"Why do you ask?" Rangabes said, his hand cautiously hovering over his scabbard.

"Shaitan," he whispered. The inn went silent and Rangabes turned to look at the men in the room. There were three of them, all fighting men from the look of it.

The sultry women slid back to their rooms and shut the doors at the mention of the word. "Shaitan," the barkeep hissed more forcefully.

"A demon? Please." Rangabes chuckled at the superstitious man.

"I do not care if you believe or not, but I will give you free room and board if you stay and guard this inn for the next couple of days at least." He kneaded his hands and his eyes darted towards the front door as if expecting attack.

"One night and one night only. I must be on my way." Rangabes crossed his arms expectantly.

"Whatever you say. A night with an extra man is better than nothing. The shaitan is due any day now."

Rangabes scoffed and made his way over to an empty seat, ignoring the other men. The barkeep hastily brought him some scraps of meat and a drink. The inn was silent but for his animalistic devouring of the food and drink. Ravenous, he immediately called for a second helping. The barkeep happily obliged, apparently happy to be doing something other than wringing his hands and staring fearfully at the door.

The three Ottomans were gripping their scimitars now, pacing about as if expecting attack right that moment. Rangabes chuckled, finishing the last of his drink and wishing that the Turkish women were still out and about. The hairs on the back of his neck suddenly stood on end, and in an instant Rangabes was on his feet with his sword drawn. He knew better than to doubt his instinct. The room grew cold as if in the dead of winter. Their breath fogged in the frigid air, and the barkeep collapsed behind the counter, muttering prayers to his god. The front door creaked open but there was nobody there. A shrill shriek rattled the walls and pierced their eardrums. Rangabes buried his head in his arms and watched one of the soldiers collapse in convulsions as blood burst forth in fountains of scarlet from both of his ears.

Grimacing, Rangabes readied his sword for whatever evil this beast wrought. The room somehow got even colder, and a wicked wind whipped through the air, tearing down the ornaments on the walls and slashing at the tables, crashing plates and dinnerware in a burst of power. One soldier, apparently deciding the battle wasn't worth fighting, made for the door as if to run and as soon as he made it to the silhouetted black frame his skin melted off like wax on a blazing candle. He liquified into a gooey mess and his skeleton clattered to the floor in a pool of black blood. The remaining soldier cried, and fled towards the rooms where the women hid, throwing open the door and slamming it shut. Rangabes took a deep breath and gripped his sword with two hands. This was the glory he had wanted. This was the stuff of myth and legend. Perhaps the strange Turkish deity on the mountaintop was real after all. He smiled at the frivolous thought and glared at the open door. The black night bled into the dim inn, but there was still nothing there.

"Will you fight me face to face, spawn of Satan?" Rangabes said, his voice hammering against the freezing and empty room.

"Ssspawn of Sssatan," a voice hissed. A serpent's whisper. "You Greeks sure have fallen far." An evil cackle sounded behind Rangabes and he spun and held his sword up to just barely block a red-taloned claw from tearing his face off.

He jumped backwards and prepared to take on the beast. It was red with two horns and had dripping half-decayed fangs. It had the hooves of a goat and the talons of a gigantic bird of prey. Most unsettlingly, it had a smooshed, swirling face of bubbling fat right in the center of its gut. The face cackled and grimaced, a black forked tongue flicking out from where its navel should have been.

"Your name? I must know who the foe is that I am about to best," Rangabes taunted, his confidence flaring as he thrust his sword forward. His thoughts flew to that of Aeneas besting Turnus, to Hercules subduing Cerberus, to Samson pulling down the pillars... he felt the heroic flowing in his veins.

"My name. My name is nameless. I belong to the rootless. I rot those who forget what it is to be. Your present time here is perfect for that. Your city will fall, my pretty little soldier, and you will die defending it. Your city will fall because it lost what once made it great. I am the terror of the forgotten past. I am the revenge of the spat-upon greats. I pluck out the blind eyes of the fallen. If you cannot see where you came from and what greatness was and is, then how can you persist? A tree without roots is rotted wood. I am Evellam."

Rangabes chuckled. He'd lowered his sword to listen to the demon prattle on while the monster's stomach face burped and gurgled irreverently. No more would he stomach this. He laughed again at the unintentional pun and thrust forward, jabbing his sword and bending his body like the swaying tree, snapping forward like a barbed whip. He flowed forth as only a river could, dancing with the demon as it ferociously swung its talons, clawing unsuccessfully for his face. His cloak was soon reduced to tatters, but he was no worse for wear other than a scratch below his left eye. He evaded the chortling demon, no longer on the offensive but shifting his tactics to that of the patient defender, waiting for the right moment for the perfect counter.

The moment came when Evellam overextended himself, swinging both claws down in an overhead slamming move which caused him to stumble forward

109

exposed. Rangabes rolled out of the way and sliced at the demon's belly, cutting the black-blooded beast in half, sending a spray of guts onto the floor as its stomach face choked in blood, crying out as it twitched until finally going silent and still. The detached torso quivered, and the demon's head glared glassy-eyed at Rangabes.

"You still will die with your city. I will arise again and again, as long as you foolish mortals forget what is great. As long as you forget what is true... what is powerful," he hissed, his voice strained and weak. Evellam smiled up at Rangabes just as his sword decapitated the shaitan. He threw the head aside and walked towards the barkeep. He banged his fist on the counter and the man cried for mercy. "Why was this... Evellam here? Why would he attack this worthless inn?"

"He... he... have mercy sir. He told me that a Greek soldier would come. He told me I must wait. I... I didn't know why or how... or even who. I got those other soldiers to defend me... but, but forgive me."

"Turkish dog." Rangabes walked away and headed for a room.

He'd earned his keep as far as he was concerned. And he couldn't deny it, he was excited at the prospect of facing more of the mythical. He was strangely honored that the demon had been waiting for him. This was what he had longed for. That woman Venia, she knew how to win his heart.

16
Divine Insanity

There is a virile madness that is life affirming and pure, greater even than the combined spirits of Dionysus and Apollo, and forming something higher, something still undefined. All great men must be mad, for to be sane is to be satisfied with death. No satisfaction, only striving. This madness, this reveling in power is to strive against the wimpy, limp-wristed modern sissy fits who slump their shoulders and bury their faces in their phones. Divine madness is found in most heroes of both the mythic and actual. A man has to be mad to make a mark. Anyone who turns his face away from the status quo and seeks glory is a madman to the plebeians. In the Eastern Orthodox Church, particularly in Russia, there were many great saints known as Fools for Christ. These men and women would wear little to no clothing, often being nude in public or in rags. It was a form of asceticism that gave up all comforts and reputation in the name of Christ. There was much power in this too, because the fools were able to call out the public for degeneracy because of their blamelessness and low position in society. One of the more well-known fools was Basil the Blessed. He would rebuke and challenge Ivan the Terrible (really should be called Ivan the Formidable but Terrible is his more well-known moniker) for not caring for the church and for his violence. Basil was essentially the only man who could speak to the Grand Prince like that. There is much power in not caring what other people think, and in embracing madness to the point of being able to speak plainly and harshly to any person.

The Maenads were female followers of Dionysus that moved about in ecstatic states of frenzy. They followed the mad god of drink himself. They danced passionately, intoxicated and sultry as they lived mad lives of passion

and power. Dionysus provided for them and made sure
their cup was always full, and they always woke up fresh
and revived. While not exactly fools for Christ, they
certainly embraced the madness of their chosen god. They
were not ashamed to live and rejoice, and because of this
they carried a mystique and power that the pencil pusher or
church lady will never know. To rejoice with fervor and
life is to be free, and in their divine madness they did not
care about the sheep clamoring beneath them. Our
movement needs women like this too, the same way in
which we need nationalist Aphrodites. Women who do not
hide in the underworld but revel in it, and because of this
they gain power and access to secrets an Odysseus would
never have access to. Madness is a useful shield against the
lower, mortal and weak controlled insanities of the leftists.
Lyssa the goddess of madness would fit the bill of leftist
insanity. Hera used the goddess to drive Hercules into
killing his own family. That is not the life-affirming
madness I speak of.

There is still one form of madness that is a bit of a
mystery, and something that has fascinated me for some
time. I'm referring to the strange case of Nietzsche's
madness. The philosopher was always a sort of mad man in
the life-affirming way that we tyrants should strive to be,
but towards the end of his sane life, he broke down at last
and became a vegetable for more than a decade before
finally dying. The commonly accepted theory is that it was
due to syphilis, but I am not so sure. Nietzsche had stated
many times throughout his works that if he couldn't work
out the right philosophy to answer the problem of nihilism
and existence in general, then it would be better for him to
go insane. Well, he managed to create some awe-inspiring
works and I think that every nationalist and tyrant alike
should read his writings, but he was unable to fully live his
conception of the Übermensch. That is, he was unable to

ever create values unattached to the soft Christian morality that informed even the most ardent atheist. He set out to do this with his book that would posthumously be released as *The Will to Power*. Most people read this book assuming it is his magnum opus but that couldn't be farther from the truth. *The Will to Power* is a great book, but hardly his best simply because it is a collection of a bunch of his drafts and thoughts put together in one book, organized after he was gone. The actual copy of *The Will to Power* he'd been working on before going insane had grocery lists in the margins, and doodles and notes that by all appearances seemed to signify his having abandoned it halfway through. The task proved too monumental in the end, and his famous last moment of clarity came (whether or not this really happened is hard to prove) when he saw a horse being whipped and he threw himself in harm's way to protect it, hugging it close.

The philosopher against pity showed pity in his last moments of sanity. I'd suggest looking up his affectionately titled *Madness Letters* that he wrote shortly after the incident, before being put into a mental institution. There seems to be something more to it all, but it is shame there is no way to know. Doctors have put forward other causes of his breakdown because he shouldn't have been able to survive so much longer after losing his senses. He had many other health problems that ailed him his whole life, so again there is no way to know for certain. I have my own theory. I think that he realized the impossibility of creating values from power and nothing else, and he realized the Sisyphean task he'd begun. And so, being true to his past words on embracing insanity if unsuccessful, he did just that. Perhaps he realized pity was not the enemy, for is there any more poetic way to end than pitying a horse of all beings, from the man who hated pity? If my theory is correct, him embracing madness and sitting in utter silence is the most Übermensch thing he could do. Perhaps he realized his error and he embraced madness in penance for his failure. That is a divine madness. If my theory were true, Nietzsche might just be the most powerful madman of all time. Otherwise, he suffered a sad death and failure, kept alive for years as an invalid. I hope my theory is true, but regardless, madness has many facets and when wielded for life, passion, glory and power, madness is the way to move above the herd and perhaps bring a few mad ones with you too.

17
Faith Worth Fighting For

For those who are religious, or those who believe that violence is antithetical to living a meaningful, good and holy life, I want to bring up a few real-world examples of men who disprove such a foolish theory. Vlad Dracula, better known as Vlad the Impaler is a man maligned by most today and very misunderstood. First, the name Dracula is a variation of Dracul, a moniker he earned through his service in the Order of the Dragon. The Order's purpose was to stop the Ottomans from advancing into Europe. When his father and brother died, he became ruler of Wallachia and won back lands from the Ottomans. There were many wars and battles, and he fought valiantly and bravely with his armies. His reign had much success and some failure, but what I want to focus on is the impaling he became so known for. The first instance was when he had Saxon villagers impaled; the villagers were under control of Vlad's half-brother and two other opponents who opposed his rule. Vlad also had Sultan Mehmed II's envoys impaled, refusing to hear the Ottoman's offer. He was never one to be on the defensive, and he attacked Ottoman territories soon after. Eventually he was dethroned and imprisoned. He managed to escape and die a worthy death in battle.

But how could a Christian man be responsible for such violent acts, you ask? For one, much of his cruelty was greatly exaggerated. Even still, he undoubtedly committed mass murders and by impaling no less (a painful way to die that involved placing a sharpened stake through the bottom and torso, extending out the head. If impalement avoided organs the person might survive several days, in constant torment, which is why such a method was considered so cruel and unusual). However, Romania came to regard Vlad as a national hero, a tyrant who was just and powerful. It is said that his tortures and punishments were done for a reason, and he was a valiant defender of his land and people against an aggressive Ottoman Empire that had desecrated and destroyed Eastern Christianity. This was a man of power, and his displays of tyranny were done to strike fear in his enemies' hearts and to defend and promote a European people. If he had acted kindly, like the soft-minded politicians of modernity, he would have been killed before ever coming to power, and his land would have been overrun by Ottomans who had no problem raping and pillaging their enemies, as Allah had no concern for the well-being of infidels. May a new Vlad rise up as a just tyrant, fighting for his people against the nauseous waves of materialistic nihilism threatening to destroy society.

Is his reign any different from St. Constantine the Great, who saw the sign of the cross over the battle field proclaiming, "In this sign you will conquer"? Real Christianity is one worth fighting and dying for. Christ never told soldiers to stop fighting. Paul had armed guards protect him. Just warfare and violence are necessary. The Old Testament is filled with ethnic cleansings commanded by God, there is no way around that. To love your neighbor, sometimes your enemy needs to be vanquished. There are plenty of other examples of warrior saints and Christian Emperors, and I implore all you Christian nationalists to not be afraid or ashamed of violence. Death and war will only be finished when the new earth comes and all evil is defeated. Until then, we must fight for truth and not let our enemies tell us how we should follow our own faith. They use popular talking points seen in mass media, but they also have never read the bible. Even if you throw the Old Testament out, Christ still whips the greedy fools desecrating the temple with usury. What peaceful hippie would wield a barbed whip, driving hordes of men out with pure power? I'm not encouraging violence or some militaristic uprising. All I'm trying to say is that we shouldn't be ashamed of a triumphant history that sometimes involved bloodshed. Christianity is not for pacifists. Do not forget, Christ died on a cross but he is returning with a sword.

18
Men of Greatness

Napoleon spent much of his youth alone, studying, reading and writing about all sorts of subjects. His goal was that of mastery. He read of the heroic, so as to apply their traits of heroism and methods of power unto his own life. He wanted to be a writer at first. He also wanted to be a nationalist on his tiny island of Corsica before shifting his gaze to France and then to the rest of Europe, and so on. Napoleon is an excellent case of seizing the moments of power offered to him and not getting down on losing out on his earlier dreams and goals. We must all refine and be ready to grab at any form of power that comes our way, accidental or not. We too can study the heroic, and I hope this book has awakened a desire in you to study mythology and heroism in cultures not bogged down by false promises of equality and weak modernity. Learn from those who have already succeeded. Napoleon was obsessed throughout his entire life with studying and learning from the feats that great men of power and heroic attributes accomplished. Might we have a Napoleon in our midst? He was no towering figure (however, his shortness is greatly exaggerated and likely the result of British propaganda) and his complexion and weight often convinced others that he was ill. But the only illness that thrived in that man was an unquenchable thirst for greatness and power. May we all drink to that, and may our thirst remain unquenched!

Study men of power, especially those who rose to absolute dominance in societies of degeneracy and decay. Napoleon and Hitler rose to absolute power despite the decadent modernity of the democracies they inhabited. And Napoleon's rise was in a failed republic that couldn't serve as a worthy replacement to the monarchy they had just rebelled against. America is a strange one, as its founding is based on the doctrine of democracy, however stilted it was in its creation. Even still, do you mean to tell me that democracy is final in America and the greater world? Will there never be a new movement at hand? Democracy is a newcomer to the world and has not been around long enough to even touch the monarchies and empires that dominated antiquity. There are other ways, some tried and some not. Authoritarianism is best for encouraging a love of country and tradition. But what form this source of order and control takes is unimportant. What matters is that we reach the point of remembrance, and only then can we move forward when we truly and rightfully have honored the past.

It can be fun to debate what political ideology is best, and who knows, maybe authoritarian policies aren't best either. But letting corporations run a country instead of a government doesn't seem like the right answer to me. Democracy, or at least a representative Republic might be the best mode of government, if and only if the intelligent and worthy were the ones who could vote. Voting shouldn't be a right, it should be an honor that must be earned. Then only the best people will be voting hopefully for the best of their country. How someone is qualified to vote is beyond me, and not worth seriously considering until we've infiltrated our current form as it is. If immigration isn't slowed, we won't be around long enough to salvage this country, no matter how stringent the voting laws become. Let's all strive together to get into power and not simply slow down the decline, but increase the country's glory and triumph long since maligned and forgotten. Our destiny was once considered manifest. Let's not only remind the herd of that destiny, but bring it to fruition with the herd at our backs and following our lead.

19

Feather and Fear
Rangabes Part II of III

The mountain loomed and the solitary Rangabes crawled up to its peak like a spider, his dragged footprints trailing behind like threads of silk. The journey had thinned his tanned face, and his sinewy muscle crept across his sunken skin like ridges and valleys of a desolate wasteland. Musala was barren and rocky.

He was glad to have finally arrived, eager as he was to test his mettle once again. Months had passed since Evellam and he was ready for another mythical beast to best.

Ascending the last few steps up the peak, he looked around and saw no monster. There was a small body of water in the distance and some striking green plant life amidst the canopy of gray that were the mountains around him.

Looking upwards, he called out to the heavens, "Am I on the right path?"

The sky shook and storm clouds blackened the horizon. Whether it was a good or bad omen, he was indifferent. He only wanted more opportunity for glory. The shaitan had left him wanting for much, much more.

"Tengri, you Turkish lie! Come down if you are real! I must have your feather or scale, whatever form you take on. I've killed your demon."

The clouds blotted out the sun, billowing out in the heavens like a sinister cloak. A black-feathered dragon soared from out of the clouds, its skin crackling with black energy as if onyx thunderbolts ran through its plumage. It glowed black like polished coal burning in blue fire. He smiled and held his sword, eagerly awaiting this Tengri.

"A pure white goose is what I expected! Or at least a snowy dragon, but this. A black beast of the storm? I will put you down like the lying dog you are. I don't care what kind of myth you've become."

Tengri, the size of Hagia Sophia herself, glided lazily down, spiraling above the lone soldier like a vulture knowing its prey was moments away from being finished.

"Come down you fowl beast. A fearful pigeon you are! Fly high with the sparrows for to near is to face death!" Rangabes waved his sword angrily, then threw his head back and cackled insanely enough to make even Tengri question the man's sanity.

Had they pushed him too far into the mythic before he'd been ready for the heroic? Had his encounter with Evellam sent him too far into the meeting place between the mythical and actual, that dreaded in-between where power and the unreal tangle together into a crackling spear point of glory—something too eternal and otherworldly for most to survive.

Rangabes watched the strange devil circling above. If a crow became a dragon, it'd probably look something like this demon. He wished he'd brought his bow, and he searched the barren mountain top for anything he could use as a ranged weapon. There was nothing but rocks on the ground, so he bent low and gathered a handful. He hurled them upwards to no avail. What was the beast waiting for? Was he waiting to see if he was worthy of fighting? He'd show this beast who was worthy!

"Tengri! Save me if you dare, and are willing to fight a battle you're destined to lose."

With a prayer to the holy Theotokos, protector of Constantinople, he leapt off of the mountain top and into the air, plummeting down to his doom. His gamble paid off as a black feathery streak slid under Rangabes before he could hit the face of rock beneath him, and he was whisked up into the heavens. His sword slipped from his grasp, and he held on as tight as he could while the beast soared straight up into the air. The demon's feathers were cold to the touch. Its back was surprisingly soft and tender beneath the purple-black plumage. The feathers served as excellent grips, but nevertheless Rangabes struggled to hang on as the wind pulled him down.

Higher Tengri flew until they were enveloped in a cloud of black. Then, like a fetus bursting forth from the womb, they shot out from the clouds and into a burning forest set aflame in an eerie pale-yellow glow. They landed in a clearing surrounded by this supernatural fire. Rangabes hopped off the beast and stared at its serpent-like face with hatred. Its eyes were glowing white-blue glaciers without pupils. It tilted its head as if waiting for some sort of sign.

"I have no sword and nowhere to go, but I have myself and myself is enough to best you."

Rangabes crouched like a stalking panther, and ducked just as Tengri's neck snapped forward and two glinting fangs snapped at his head. He dove out of the way and rolled to his feet. Running in circles, diving and dodging... there was nothing he could do to harm the beast, not without his sword. He felt something scalding hot in his pocket. Who had put it there? The woman! Venia had given him the dagger just before mentioning the quest; he was a fool to forget! The double-sided dagger she'd claimed came from the mystery cult of Crete celebrating death and fertility. A death cult dagger on one side, fertility cult dagger on the other: fused as one to form the ultimate weapon transcending ceremony to slay the largest of beasts. This was the weapon to bring about a new mythic age! This was the dagger to conquer Tengri.

Rangabes ducked the biting serpent head again and yanked out the dagger with a flourish and stuck it through the beast's chin. Its head fell limp and he climbed up its neck, dragging the dagger through its feathers as he ran across its back and down through its tail, all the while leaving a fine line of spurting black blood behind him. Slicing off several feathers, he went around to the beast's head and cut out its two fangs for an added treasure. He didn't see any scales, but he hoped that adding the beast's fangs would do.

The yellow flames around him roared with fury. He gave them no attention; his eyes were transfixed on the fallen god before him. A brilliant white glow like that of the sun burst from the dragon's corpse, and a glowing black dog emerged from the feathers. It barked approvingly at Rangabes and shot into the air—the reverse of a falling star. The yellow fire suddenly ceased and the sky turned to the black of night and only then did Rangabes realize that the shining star above was none other than the legendary Dog Star, Sirius. Rangabes shook his head, stuffing his trophies into his pockets. He made his way back to the road, ready to return to the woman with many questions to be answered.

20
Attuned Whole

You ever hear how females are supposed to be in tune with their emotions, and that it is weak for men to express them? Well I agree, but only to an extent. Man should only express his powerful and vulnerable emotions to those he trusts. The great Aeneas was not ashamed to weep when the right moment called for it. Christ wept over Jerusalem. I say no matter the gender, we should try to experience all the emotions, as much as possible and in a yes-saying manner. Emotions that reveal vulnerability should only be shared with those whom you are closest with. But do not bottle them up, as a man filled with turmoil is not one fit to lead and serve his people. If you share these emotions with those whom you love, you will be better prepared to control yourself and make smart decisions in strenuous moments. Knowing these emotions help you better know yourself and improve your prowess at being in control and a man of action. A man who fully knows himself will not be afraid in moments of life and death: the clarity not of an emotionless mind, but a mind that knows emotion and looks at the emotion calmly. Make sure to feel the full gambit of emotions every day. Cry. Laugh. Dance. Console. All the emotions you can think of. Do not force it, but seek out meaningful engagements that will bring out these emotions in you. An emotionless man is a robot. An emotional man is a fool. An emotion-attuned man is a worthy ally. The emotion-breathed existence is one worth pursuing, as long as you continue to control each breath with deep inhales and long exhales. Never stop breathing, and do not hyperventilate.

21
Systemic Possession

I read of Daedalus and see the USA in part of his story. Daedalus built his legendary labyrinth to hold the Minotaur captive. The labyrinth was impossible to escape, and even the clever inventor himself couldn't escape it. Well, eventually this gigantic system he made to hold a monster in check was his own prison. He and his son Icarus were thrown into that infernal labyrinth and trapped. He'd fallen prey to his own creation! Yes, he was able to escape through ingenuity, and yes, his son flew too close to the sun. But can you not see the parallels? The USA is essentially Daedalus, i.e. trapping itself inside a system with a monster of its own creation. Wings aren't enough, as we'll need to withstand a lot more heat than the sun. We should follow the thread (like Theseus) of history and escape before it is too late. Theseus came into the maze and killed the sleeping minotaur by holding a thread and dropping it so he did not get lost and lose his direction.

There is a thread of greatness that binds us tyrants to the heroic. We need to look at the history of the powerful and consider what those powerful men of the past might do in the labyrinth that is the USA of today. The longer we suffer this system, the closer the Minotaur gets to devouring us. If we continue to cede power in tolerant stagnation, there'll be nothing left of our rotted corpse for even the Minotaur to eat. Daedalus once reigned over his maze, before being forced to flee. Who really is in power now? Make the labyrinth your own. Become King Minos. Do not let a Daedalus fly free with the secrets of your maze. A vulture will remain circling carrion, no matter how lively that carrion might look. I can see the vultures descending, but we have time yet to turn another way. But Daedalus as a brilliant inventor and wise innovator is an archetype we need to pursue. Elon Musk is the most famous innovator today, and he is by no means a leftist shill. He is open to ideas of nationalism and dreams of colonizing space. Men with financial power and innovation and fearlessness combined are rare. I do not care how he got his money or how he takes advantage of the system— am I not imploring you nationalists to do the same? Elon Musk will be on the side that allows him to innovate. We as King Minos do not need to trap him, we only need to encourage him with the freedom to experiment. But we must get that power first by exploiting the system. This labyrinth can be apprehended and used for our own machinations. Let's follow that thread, and infiltrate the maze until the Minotaur's monstrous form is ours to behold. We needn't wake the sleeping giant. We become the giants ourselves when we slit the old leviathan's snoring throat. Its blood belongs to us. The monster has grown fat and we must use this infernal maze to become lean, and the monstrous will be as nothing to us new Minotaurs. Nationalism will then be at the center of our labyrinth.

Myths are rich with inspiration and tales of both power and weakness. Much can be learned and reapplied to our struggles both individually and collectively. With that said, I ask: have you heard of Bellerophon and his golden saddle? Bellerophon was a slayer of beasts, before Hercules but on the same level. Bellerophon lived quite the charmed life. He was so naturally heroic and alpha that he earned the favor of Athena and coaxed her into giving him the mighty and untamable Pegasus as his steed. She also gave him a golden saddle to place onto Pegasus's back which would help calm him. (Quick aside: Perseus is often portrayed as riding Pegasus but it was the fault of classical scholars who confused him with Bellerophon, and because of that mistake, people still assume it was Perseus who rode Pegasus but that is false). So, Bellerophon was able to ride

Pegasus and the two of them found success after success together as heroes only matched perhaps by the legendary Hercules, and the brave Perseus. I don't want to go into too much detail regarding his story (he slayed the Chimera!) but instead focus on a certain aspect of it. What we need to look at here is the simplicity in the strategy of power that is: continual success. As Trump says: "We're going to win so much you'll get tired of winning!" If you keep succeeding in whatever it is that the powers that be set out for you, they will give you more and more agency and freedom to use power as you see fit.

It is a simple and most effective way to win over the trust of supposed enemies and to gain power to wield from the devil himself. But one cannot get too big-headed and forget gifts and friends. One cannot be so overconfident that one tries to fly to Mount Olympus and ignore allies. Do you want to become a pariah, alone and away from destiny and power? Do you know what happened to Bellerophon? He grew so overconfident after years of successful questing that he tried to fly to Olympus and join the gods. Pegasus refused, trying to warn him of his ridiculous hubris. He did not listen and ultimately fell from the soaring steed's back and into deadly thorn bushes that blinded him. He died alone and destitute. Listen to your allies. Gain success but be patient. Don't have too much success either or you might be singled out as dangerous. A delicate balance must be met. To rush ahead is to crumble. Charlottesville anybody? Where is the so-called Alt-right today? Fragmented and full of itself. Have success within the system, gain Athena-like allies but do not offend such powerful figures. Patience and virtue are key. Success comes to the one who bides his time, procures a golden saddle and rides the system of power unto eventual victory. To ignore warnings from the system itself is to be chewed up and spit out by that same system you were trying to infiltrate and destroy. Ride the system out until it sputters in exhaustion and becomes yours to tame.

22
The Quest for the Golden Fleece

Jason and the Argonauts, and their quest for the
Golden Fleece, is a myth worth telling again and again. It is
an epic story of heroism and tragedy, worthy and ripe for
analysis and application to our own quest for glory and
power. If we follow the path of Hercules in his labors and
Jason in his quest, we not only will achieve power but we
will receive a glory known to few mortal men; in a sense,
to follow the mythical heroic path of triumph all the way to
the end is to become gods. Divinity—as outlandish as it
may sound—is not as impossible as the sissy fits of our age
think.

The sissy fits roll their balls of dung up the hills and
celebrate their increasing degeneracy while decrying
anything that is worth memorializing and celebrating. We
are not the Sisyphus that is modernity, pushing and pulling
filth up a hill as if it is some precious object worth
celebrating as sacred. The idols of today are feces to the
heroes of myth. We don't pretend that crap is anything but,
and we see that it certainly isn't worth protecting let alone
exalting. Degeneracy is weakness and the will to death,
which requires an obvious hatred for anything and
everything that shines forth life. To the bugmen and sissy
fits, and to the entire globohomo regime, the life-affirming
man of power and beauty is the negation of all that is
sacred to their cult of death.

Let us follow the path of the heroic; divinity on
earth is found in the power and glory of saying yes to
becoming. To never stop is to become a godman now. No
clouds are needed when the earth and its insect-infested
cities bow to the greatness that is the mythical and heroic.
A tyrant is a god to the weak. When weakness is considered
greatness, a tyrant is even more of a god because he can

destroy the deceit and recreate the mythic. There are enough dunghills. There is only one Mount Olympus, and it is waiting to be ascended once more by true tyrants worthy of godhood. So, let us now examine Jason and his mighty band of heroes, and may we be inspired and forewarned of the glories and treacheries that await the hero.

The beginning of this story is not so important, but only necessary to explain the origin of the Golden Fleece itself. Essentially, a conniving queen jealous of other children whom she viewed as capable of taking the throne, hatched a complicated plan to starve the inhabitants of her land so that the people would cry for the child in question to be sacrificed. The child's name was Phrixus and he was only spared by the prayers of his desperate mother. Hermes answered her prayers and sent a majestic golden ram that whisked the boy away into the air along with his sister (who perished on the journey by falling off and drowning) to a faraway land.

King Æëtes welcomed the boy into his city. As a token of appreciation, Phrixus sacrificed the golden ram to Zeus and offered the king the golden fleece, which he gladly accepted. However, things were not all as well back in Greece. Phrixus's uncle in Greece was the rightful king of the land but he was being usurped by a man named Pelias. This uncle had a son named Jason, and this is where the story really gets going as we are introduced to the hero.

Also, don't ask how the golden ram came into existence. Zeus and his bestiality again... which is why I'm on the side of Kronos but that's for later analysis. The great Titan did devour his children after all which was a sign of his weakness and pathetic fear, but before that he had been a being of pure and worthy power. Zeus is conniving and not trad at all; he turns himself into a swan just to bang a tradthot, and that's just one instance among many other where he banged from animal form. Zeus even takes on the female form. He is desperate for coochie, while Kronos scoffs at the weak females unworthy of his attention.

Forgive me, I got a little side tracked but there can be no room for degeneracy in the reawakening heroism of masculinity. I stand by this claim: the most masculine thing a man can do is to beat his sexual will into submission and become a volcel. The next most masculine action a man can do is to father beautiful children with a beautiful wife. There is no room for thottery and degeneracy. Don't be cuckolded—Napoleon even was! He should have stayed celibate instead of letting that whore Josephine use him and turn him into such a cuck. Maybe he couldn't win a naval battle because all his semen was spilled on the boots of Josephine, as she laughed and banged other men while he jerked off at the thought of the slightest attention from her. Thankfully, Jason is no Napoleon when it comes to women (though he has his Zeus-like moment in the end). But regarding the myth, let's refocus on Jason and the false king named Pelias.

Jason is rightfully annoyed and angry that Pelias has stolen the throne for himself. Oracles prophesied to Pelias that Jason would one day take the throne, so Pelias devised an impossible quest for Jason to complete, telling him he could take the throne once he succeeded bringing back the golden fleece. Jason immediately accepted, and he hungered for the glory and power of the heroic quest set before him. He gathered heroes together from all over the land, masculine shouts of promised glory and triumph ringing through the streets. Fair maidens swooned as Jason formed a glorious tribe called the Argonauts, named for riding his ship called Argo.

Here is a list of the men that made up the crew of the Argonauts: the **Boreads** who could fly and were sons of the North Wind, divine **Hercules** before his 12 labors had been finished, **Philoctetes** who was the son of a king and a famed archer that fought in the Trojan war, **Peleus** who was a hero in his own right and the father of Achilles, **Telamon** who was a great fighter that took part in many heroic ventures such as helping Hercules with one of his labors and fighting in the Trojan war as well as fathering Ajax, **Orpheus**, the legendary musician who could win the favor of even the fiercest of gods through his unmatched singing and lyre playing, **Castor and Pollux** who were inseparable twin brothers who rode horses of foam on top of waves and eventually were turned into constellations so as to remain immortal together forever, **Atalanta** who was a fierce, volcel huntress wedded only to the hunt for glory (the goddess of the hunt, Artemis, made Atalanta her worthy champion), **Meleager** who was a great hero and host of the Calydonian Boar hunt (I'm guessing he also knew how to throw crazy parties), and **Euphemus** who could walk on water and was the son of Poseidon.

It is interesting to note that Atalanta was likely the only female aboard, and it is possible that she snuck on destroying any hopes of masculine brotherhood if not for her faith and skill. She had Artemis's protection, and as a chaste virgin she had no interest in sexual favors among those handsome heroes. Now, if the typical female had stumbled on she would not have been able to resist such masculine charm. What makes Atalanta special is her faith in serving her god and her disdain for chasing after the easy things in life. She was volcel and a priestess of the similarly virginal Artemis, and the men soon accepted her as their own when she earned her stripes. Normally I'd advise against including females in such a masculine endeavor as they only complicate things—when there is only one of them and many testosterone-fueled men without a sexual outlet, something bad is bound to happen and a wedge might be driven through the tribe.

Atalanta also beat Peleus in wrestling, in front of a large crowd during funeral games. She had to prove her might, but might and power wouldn't be enough alone for a woman to be allowed to participate in such a quest. What was enough was the fact that Artemis held her champion in such high esteem, and the men respected those worthy of serving the gods. Joan of Arc is another woman who fulfilled such a role. Her success, faith and strength were enough to make her "one of the boys". There was no fooling around sexually with her. I do think there are rare cases where such women exist, and if one such as Atalanta wants to join you and your men, ask her to wrestle. If she wins and declares her victory for the divine, invite her in. If she claims the victory for herself, run as far away as possible. Prideful women cannot be trusted.

With the crew together, the Argonauts set out on their quest for the golden fleece aboard their massive galley the Argo. The first island they stopped at was called Lemnos, the ultimate feminist paradise. On Lemnos there were only women as the wives had all killed their husbands on the island. The reason is quite hilarious, as the women did not worship Aphrodite and the goddess punished them by making the women smell unbearable to their husbands. Think of the parallels! The hairy feminists of today stink and worship no higher truth but themselves in their constant outrage at decency and strength. Most feminists want straight men dead anyways, especially the white ones. In modernity a goddess cursing them would be the government encouraging their degenerate destruction of toxic masculinity. They are already on the way there. But the myth gets even juicier, as the Argonauts were disgusted at the crazy cat women of Lemnos and they took concubines from the neighboring Thrace instead. The women of Lemnos despite their hatred of masculinity couldn't help but scream in jealous rage. One only has to imagine the modern feminist promoting fat acceptance and calling any fit male a member of the patriarchy and an oppressor. They say this because they can get no dick!

The Argonauts were real heroic pirates who embraced the manliness of a seafaring life. I don't doubt that the concubines came willingly, once the golden men stepped on their shore. The Argonauts being such testosterone-fueled heroes could not resist at least exploring the feminist island as it still had women there after all. They spent a few days there and impregnated the lot of them. It turns out that the man-hating women couldn't resist the manliness of the Argonauts. That is why I beg of you modern men, work out and pursue the heroic! Many women will come to the side of Chad, no matter how much they claim to despise him.

But there's another aspect here: Hercules refused to take part in the intercourse with the women of Lemnos. He viewed them as disgusting and beneath him for their sin of cleansing the island of males. Hercules had sex with many, many women without any qualms but the feminists he apparently knew to avoid. I can imagine he and Atalanta standing aboard their ship, refusing to set foot on such polluted soil. I'm sure Atalanta had a good laugh at the hypocrites of Lemnos, and continued training and studying. There are two sides of this coin. Was Hercules right, or were the rest of the Argonauts correct? Some say you should avoid interacting romantically with any feminist at all. I agree. The women of Lemnos are a feminist's dreamworld, where men who don't like them are slaughtered in their sleep (which is why none were left, so undesirable did these women become). Hercules could have any woman on the planet, including various goddesses, so why would he debase himself with those murderous creatures?

On the other hand, Jason slept with the queen and had twins. He no doubt converted the queen to the way of tyranny, once she understood his power. But the rest of the Argonauts slept with who knows how many of the women on that island. Maybe they treated the murderers like the prostitutes they were, or maybe they tried to find the highest quality women. I do think it is possible to turn a feminist into a Stacey, but I think it is better to find a normal girl that is beautiful and not fully perverted by feminist nonsense. Hercules was eager to continue on the quest for glory and the Argonauts finally relented and went on their way. Also worth noting is the creation of a new race from the Argonauts' copulation with the feminist murderers of Lemnos. There is a lesson here that I do not think needs to be explicitly said. How do you think such a race would fare? The fathers leave and crazy mothers curse them. No identities. Only confusion and hatred for Argonauts. See the parallel? Even if they had stayed, no doubt the children would still come to resent the foreign Argonauts or perhaps better put in the more popular term of our current age—colonizers. Usually it's the other way around with foreign men stealing our own women, turning the women into the crazed killers of Lemnos.

Moving onwards, the Argonauts dined with King Kyzikos who graciously hosted them. They then headed on to Bear Mountain where the six armed and savage race of giants called the Gegenees dwelled. The Argonauts landed near the forest and the majority of them went in search of supplies, leaving just a few behind to guard the Argo. Seeing these few men, the Gegenees figured it'd be easy to overpower them. Of course, they didn't anticipate one of those men being Hercules, who easily killed the giants with his quiver of arrows and large club. They set sail again and had to stop once more and send some men to repair a broken oar as well as get some more supplies.

Hercules's servant Hylas went alone to gather water. Hercules himself was gathering wood to repair the broken oar and Hylas was left alone for the moment. Hylas was so excruciatingly handsome that he attracted several water nymphs who pulled him into the river to have him for themselves and he vanished without a trace. Hercules became overly distraught and guilt-ridden, and left the Argonauts behind. Some accounts say he had already begun his labors before joining the quest for the fleece, and he continued them thereafter, abandoning the quest perhaps feeling responsible for the loss suffered. Other accounts say he fled in hysterical madness, and his 12 labors came soon after. Regardless, he departed and was a member of the Argonauts no longer, a devastating blow for the hopes of completing the already impossible task. To make matters worse, during the night they accidentally went the wrong way and ended up skirmishing with King Kyzikos and his men. The Argonauts slew most of them, including the king for whom they held a funeral—the man who had just before hosted them so graciously.

As can be clearly observed, this stage in their journey was a rough one that included killing those who aided them in friendly fire, and losing men as well as arguably the most powerful member of the crew (though they'd all dispute that, being heroes in their own individual rights, despite Hercules's impending godhood). How can this abject instance of failure be of use to nationalists today? Well first, I think an obvious point to take away from this is the importance of being gracious to one another. King Kyzikos was an excellent host, and he showered the Argonauts with wine, gifts and women. This is something nationalists need to work on—the aspect of community-building. Organizing get-togethers where activism and politics are put on the backburner with a focus on comradery instead, is crucial. Community needs to be built and established. To be brothers in arms one needs to be a brother first. Too often we forget that.

There are groups forming that are doing things such as this, and it's encouraging to see real-life networks being established where families are being cared for and lifelong bonds are being forged. That is what is required to make a dent in the degeneracy that we face today. Whether reactionary or religious, or both—I think there needs to be groups of like-minded individuals and allies, where the atheist reactionary can host the religious one, and despite any disagreements, they each enjoy each other's company. Those who focus on their own becoming as well as the nation's have more in common with each other than the unwashed degenerates that pollute much of this world. The flip-side of that is riding into darkness and slaying those who you thought were on your side, just as the Argonauts did against King Kyzikos and his men. The Alt-right's implosion and bickering were pathetic. When gathering together, if things go wrong at least hold some form of recapitulation afterwards. The Argonauts held a funeral—it doesn't undo the damage but it is better than turning their backs and acting as if nothing were wrong.

There are many different kinds of nationalists that need to become tyrants, dominating the self to dominate the future of this nation. Our differences now are almost nonexistent when compared to the Tartarus-sized black deep that separates us from the modern fool in power, and the powerless pawn who doesn't have an original thought of his or her or better yet—its—own. When a man is lost, or a trusted member betrays our cause, we cannot lose hope like Hercules and turn solely to our own labors. Man needs to fight for himself by fighting for the whole. To tyrannize existence, the individual must better himself through his work for the whole. The two are not mutually exclusive. Now if you're in such a rut that you're say... obese or

137

jobless or drowned in debt, etc., by all means get yourself in order. If you're already level-headed and in decent shape, you improve yourself most while improving your lot with others and for others. That is nationalism! For Hercules, his labors were put on hold for this epic quest with companions, and they did not need to be returned to because of one setback. Do not abandon the cause for glorification of self. The Argonauts kept rowing. Our ship cannot be abandoned for if she sinks, there will be nothing left to return to.

Returning to the story, the Argonauts kept sailing until they ran into a starving, tortured prophet of sorts named Phineas. Zeus sent Harpies—bird-like half-human female monsters that were known as the hounds of Zeus—to starve him to death. Iris, the goddess of the rainbow, requested that the Argonauts help Phineas, and the mighty heroes took pity on the prophet and saved him. The Boreads, the fleet-footed sons of the North Wind, flew into the air and chased the Harpies away. In return, Phineas revealed the way through the treacherous Symplegades (the Clashing Rocks). The Argonauts managed to sail through the Clashing Rocks by releasing a dove that just barely made it through, losing some tail feathers in the process. Phineas had said if the dove made it then they must follow immediately; if it did not then all hope was lost. They rowed powerfully after the dove and made it through as the rocks slammed together, scraping their boat but doing no real damage. From then on, the rocks joined together and the passage was forever made safe because of their triumph.

At long last they had reached the distant land of Colchis. This was where Phrixus had originally fled and given the gold fleece to King Æëtes. King Æëtes was not all too pleased to see Jason, and right away he devised three impossible tasks for him to complete in order to receive the golden fleece. The tasks were threefold: plow a field with a fire-breathing ox that he had to yoke and control himself, plant dragon's teeth in the field which would then sprout an army of deadly warriors called Spartoi, and finally to defeat the always vigilant, never sleeping dragon that guarded the golden fleece. Jason was extremely discouraged hearing the tasks, but knew there was no other way.

Hera, who'd been watching over the Argonauts, grew worried at the difficulties Jason would have to face. She got the idea to persuade Aphrodite to get Eros to shoot Medea, the King's daughter, with one of his arrows to make her fall madly in love with Jason. Not only was Medea the daughter of the king, but she was also a borderline goddess with her magical power, though still mortal. She was the granddaughter of Helios and niece of Circe, and her lineage played an important role in her future endeavors, but more immediately in aiding Jason.

Eros shot his arrow and Medea was caught in the snare of love's unrelenting bite. She didn't want to act against her father's wishes but her sudden desire for Jason was too much to overcome and she reached out to him. It turned out that he was just as attracted to her as she was to him. To aid him with his tasks, she gave him oils for his skin that would make him temporarily invulnerable to the flames from the ox. Regarding the army that sprouted from the dragon's teeth, she told him a simple secret: if he threw a rock just so in their midst when they sprang forth from the ground, they would turn on each other and slay themselves as they'd be unable to figure out where the rock came from. For the dragon, Medea gave him a potent potion to spray that would put the dragon to sleep. With her aid, Jason easily accomplished the tasks that had previously had him despairing so hard that he had been ready to die.

Of course, King Æëtes was not going to let him get away with the fleece that easily. Yet, the king was still unaware of his daughter's treachery and she used his misplaced trust to distract him as Jason and the Argonauts fled with the golden fleece in their possession. Her brother Apsyrtus led a fleet of ships to chase after the Argonauts, and Medea joined Apsyrtus aboard his ship. Still ever loyal to Jason and possessed by a love that only Eros could cause, she killed her brother and threw the pieces of his body into the sea. King Æëtes stopped the fleet to gather the pieces of his body for burial, and Medea boarded the Argo before her father could stop her. Distraught as he was, he turned back to his home in defeat and darkness.

There is another version, which paints Medea in a less sinister light, where she tricked her brother into meeting with Jason who then cut his toes and fingers off after killing him. Why he cut the fingers and toes off a dead corpse, I am not quite sure. Regardless, she killed her brother and chose Jason so either way it's not all that different, and in the end, Jason left Colchis with the golden fleece in his possession.

A lot happened on that final leg of his journey to Colchis, and during the whole act of getting the golden fleece in the first place. I think something that strikes me as really clear here is that it helps to have friends in high places. Yes, I know there's nothing groundbreaking in such an obvious statement, but having friends in high places—especially for nationalists in America today—means having friends that mostly disagree with the majority of what we believe. So, to have these friends, we need to be somewhat all right with the status quo. What! How dare I utter such nonsense, why even write this book? Why infiltrate if the status quo is fine? Take a few deep breaths and consider the current state of affairs.

Trump has shifted power for the moment to the right and to an odd civic but not quite civic nationalism that is nativist without a hard center to ground it on other than

MAGA, which essentially just means that America was great at some point in the fuzzy past for reasons unknown. Those MAGA people are our higher-ups. Do you think Hera is fully on board with Jason? She kills mortals all the time and tortures them if Zeus even looks at them for a second. For heaven's sake, she tortured Hercules in despicable ways, yet him joining the Argonauts didn't even affect her care for Jason and his crew.

The really intriguing part is that Hera sent Iris, the messenger goddess of rainbows, to help Jason against Zeus—the ultimate higher-up of all higher-ups! If we prove ourselves worthy, someone in power might just lower his head into our ranks to request our support. And if we provide support that is successful... well the reward is obvious: we'll be told how to make it through the Clashing Rocks of the power system. We'll be able to get through the political, economic and cultural realms. We'll send our dove first, our offer of goodwill; sometimes the dove will be slain. Many times, most definitely. And if it does make it through, feathers missing or not, we have to follow that goodwill full steam ahead and enter through the treacherous channel. Once we make it into the positions of power, joining our higher-up friends, even if only at the lower rungs, we will have then brought nationalism into the mainstream to such a point that we cannot be sidelined simply as hateful and unimportant.

We'll still be told that our inherent evil is unwelcome and unsustainable, but it will no longer really be so as public support shifts more and more to our side. With enough support, the Clashing Rocks will be sealed and our battered bodies triumphant, the gatekeepers no longer there! That is how the rock can be made whole and the passage safe. But we must first accept the system as is, offer goodwill to those who ask and not to those who would disavow if caught speaking with us—do not forget

Trump did not disavow the Charlottesville Unite the Right protestors even as everyone called for him to do it. He called out both sides. That is the kind of man and higher-up we offer our goodwill towards, and we should always be vigilant and ready for when they lower their heads and ask for our help. We can play the role of Cerberus.

And looking closer at the Phineas situation and the harpies torturing him, there are a few lessons there, some obvious and some not. We should take action to help those less fortunate than ourselves, and not only because it looks good (it most certainly does) but because to be a nationalist is to care for your own. That starts with the weak and the hurting, the starved and the tortured. The imprisoned. Phineas could not leave and was cursed by Zeus because of his knowledge of future events. When he set his hounds on the weak, those foul media harpies cawing and clawing, we must stand tall. Think of the old woman harassed by media in her own home for being a Trump supporter. Think of the cultural hounds coming for every conservative and dissident point of view. If someone knocks off a MAGA hat, step in and knock that someone's head off. I do not condone violence but if it is in self-defense or to protect others, it is worth the cost. Just make sure that if you are attacked, that somehow you can get it on film so you are not made unfairly an example of by our soft court system.

The harpies are the media. The harpies are the mainstream culture. The harpies are the hounds of groupthink. Do not run from them. Stand tall and fly into the air like the Boreas brothers, chasing the hounds off with a love for this country that is impossible to tarnish. There are still sane people here, who are tired of the political games that lack empathy for the everyday person. The left is growing insane and is desperate to cling to its waning power, no matter how nasty and deceitful they need to get. This puts the decent folk in an awkward position, and our lofty goodwill and care for them won't simply chase the harpies away, it will be their salvation. Like Phineas, they will be able to eat again—only for them it will not be food but a feast on purpose and meaning that in the political realm can only be found in nationalism.

Colchis itself, and King Æëtes's reluctance and impossible tasks, are interesting when considered through the lens of modernity. If even Jason got depressed after making it that far with so many strong allies and supporters around him, it is okay to black pill every now and then. Mourn when there is cause to mourn. Being white pilled 24/7 is unhealthy and inauthentic. Don't lie to yourself or others. But at the same time, mourn with the knowledge that you will still move forward no matter the risk. Jason was prepared to die, he couldn't have known that Hera was going to get Medea to help him. On an interesting note, Hera (Jason's higher-up connection) persuaded other higher-ups, i.e. Aphrodite and Eros, to aid them, winning unlikely and unexpected support in the process.

You never know what successful networking might bring. You may find people diametrically opposed to everything you stand for, suddenly aiding you because someone else persuaded them to with the kind of power only a true higher-up can wield. Really, it was Jason's black-pilling that moved Hera to act. Sometimes, venting the negative sides of truth out into the public can act more powerfully and persuasively than a deceitful, fantastical white pill that is actually a yellow pill (yellow representing the vacant smiley face that pretends everything is all right all the time). There'll always be a symbolic King Æëtes with impossible tasks to overcome in the never-ending quest for power. We can truthfully mourn this, but then we must dust off our feet and keep moving forward knowing what we do is not in vain, for even if it fails and America collapses, there will always be a space for tyrants to

143

tyrannize. The important part is that we keep moving, no matter how far we get pushed off the path to power. Sometimes a new path needs to be made.

But how do we get a Medea, even if higher-ups come to our aid (which is unlikely in the current climate)? In our case, we do possess the divine arrows of Eros. Jason could woo many a woman (don't forget the queen of Lemnos), but he needed Eros to win over the power and beauty of Medea, especially considering that she was naturally opposed to him because of her allegiance to her father. We must woo alluring and divine women like Medea. If we work out and make ourselves heroic and handsome, opposing beauty will be unable to resist the divine arrow of Eros that we can and must possess. The beautiful on the left will join our ranks, the right made irresistible. The reason why we possess these arrows for ourselves and Jason did not is actually quite simple: in his day and age heroism and perfection were expected. In our day, heroism and beauty are spat upon and discouraged. There are few heroes, even fewer beautiful ones. We have the power if we want to pursue it, because for us, beauty and heroism are missing in our glory-starved culture.

Win beautiful women to our side by being beautiful yourself. That is the running theme of this whole book, really. We possess the arrow and Jason didn't, yet he managed. We can skip the middleman and attack aesthetics head on with our own already superior ones. The left has worse art, architecture, culture, fitness and beauty. The right—nationalists especially—are the real aesthetic ones because beauty matters, and nationalists care the most for beauty because that is what makes a civilization, a nation and this world, better, even if at the expense of the unequal. Hierarchy is real and it matters too. The success of Jason was due to the aid of Medea. Getting beautiful women to fall in love with us can and should be used as a weapon to burn away the degeneracy through classical transformation. Imagine if the Kardashians became trad? Imagine if *insert beautiful celebrity here* suddenly spoke of traditional values, powerful men and expressed admiration for violent heroes of old. If you destroy their vapidity and materialism by showing them the real nationalist beauty of powerful men with heroic physiques, then I think it possible that they'd give us more influence and tips as it were, to complete the impossible task of transforming our degenerate country into a tyrannical aesthetic kingdom. It can be saved from the mire of nihilism, but it is bogging itself deeper in the slime every day. And like Medea showed, women can be vicious for their men and willing to turn on their handlers, no matter how much they loved their old connections. This savagery can be wielded powerfully if put to the right use. Beauty and sexual appeal win much goodwill with the herd!

And there are a few quick takeaways from King Æëtes's tasks in and of themselves. If you sow powerful seeds of discord and discussion, warriors can spring up from the muddled masses to be used accordingly. Throw the rock to make them think their enemies are one of the identity groups that shares in the same degenerate leftist nihilism as the warriors themselves. Pit the different identity groups that are supposedly on the same side against each other (this has somewhat happened on its own with Black Lives Matter and white homosexuals). Be careful though, they might just as easily attack the seed planter himself if not distracted and redirected right away. The mob rule of the rabble always destroys the great, powerful hero that is alone. Even our own can turn on us at any moment! Always be a step ahead, never simply react but prepare. Be proactive and throw the rock first, and be sure to aim it in right place. Bad throws can be just as—if not more—destructive.

145

Dragon's teeth are dangerous, but the more dangerous the seed the more powerful the potential crop might be, which goes both ways. Cover yourself in coconut oil too! Flames of the ox are like insults thrown at us. But if insults are wrong because our strength and beauty is so intoxicating, we can easily commandeer the bull because few people can resist golden skin and supple muscles. And for the sleepless dragon that is our nation, we can put it to rest with the right tonic of truth, might, and most importantly, a heroic aesthetic that is substantive and meaningful along with alluring optics.

The return journey for the Argonauts was not a simple one, and once again the crew of heroes had to face more difficulties. To begin with, Zeus cursed the Argonauts because of Medea's savagery regarding the grisly death of her brother at her own hand. He sent violent storms that greatly impeded the journey home and the ship was unable to be steered safely in the right direction, and was ultimately blown off course. To remedy this, the Argo (the ship itself) prophesied aloud and told them they needed to seek purification for their evils from the nymph Circe on the island Aeaea. They were able to be cleansed by Circe and they continued onwards now in the right direction with the storms settled and Zeus's wrath appeased.

The Argonauts then had to pass through the Sirens abode. No mortal could resist their songs that intoxicated a man with a desire to leave everything behind and come to them with reckless abandon. However, the Sirens didn't anticipate the famed musician Orpheus being on board. The great artist could silence even a god with his divine music. Orpheus played his lyre as loud and powerfully as he could, his music overpowering the Sirens' song in beauty and volume, allowing the Argo to pass through safely.

When the ship neared Crete, the giant bronze automaton named Talos sought to sink the Argo by hurling large boulders at it. To stop the bronze man, Medea cast a calming spell on him and attacked his only weakness—a single blood vessel cast in protective bronze that went from his ankle to his neck. Once he was calmed, Medea and the crew destroyed his blood vessel and Talos was vanquished. At long last, the Argonauts journey was coming to a close, but the troubles were not yet over for Jason and Medea.

Now returned to his home, Jason worried about his father Aeson's age and health. He asked Medea to take a few years from his own life and to give them to his father. Instead she took Aeson's own blood and invigorated it with herbs before putting it back, thus rejuvenating him. But Jason wasn't satisfied yet. He still wanted his vengeance against the false king Pelias, the man who'd sent Jason on the quest for the fleece in the first place. Jason implored Medea to use sorcery to slay Pelias. The perfect opportunity soon presented itself. The king's daughters, having seen Medea's power after healing Aeson, asked her to do the same for their father Pelias. She showed them how you could chop someone up into pieces and throw them into a cauldron with just the right number of herbs to heal and prolong life. She demonstrated the ritual's power by using the oldest ram in their flock. The ram came out of the cauldron as a vigorous and healthy lamb. The daughters immediately told their father what happened and he agreed to partake in the ritual, so great was his desire to prolong his life.

Medea cut him up and threw him in the cauldron but neglected to use herbs, and the king died, granting Jason his long-awaited revenge at last. Not surprisingly, Medea and Jason were forced to flee the city in exile, but they found a new home in Corinth. Once settled in Corinth, Jason married a beautiful maiden named Creusa who was the king of Corinth's daughter. Medea felt betrayed as she and Jason had already been married and he himself had promised that there would never be another woman, and that he'd love her forever. Medea asked Jason how he could do such a thing after all the help and love she'd given him. He retorted that she only helped because Eros shot her with his arrow, and that he should thank the gods and not her. Medea wasn't one to lie down and give up, so she sought her own revenge against Creusa. She gifted the unlucky maiden with a dress that burst into flames if put on. Creusa, none the wiser, accepted the gift and put it on excitedly. She was burned alive. Creon, the king of Corinth, tried to save his burning daughter but ended up dying along with her after the unholy flames consumed him as well. Medea then killed her two children she had by Jason, fearing that they'd be made slaves or murdered by Jason out of retaliation. Before Jason could find her, she fled the palace by a chariot led by dragons. Her grandfather Helios had been watching over her and had sent the chariot to help her escape. Alone and bitter, Jason took the throne of Corinth unopposed and became king. Hera cursed him because of what he had done to Medea in breaking his oaths of love he'd made to her. He ended up dying in a state of melancholy and loneliness, dying ironically under the rotting bow of his old ship Argo. While he slept on its dusted deck, it collapsed on him, killing him instantly.

      If we look at the numerous obstacles that Jason faced on the return home, we can see the importance of staying pure. Even if momentarily succumbing to degeneracy, we must do whatever we can to get out of it, or our nation will face storms worse than what Zeus could ever throw at us. An interesting aspect of the return is the Argo—the ship itself speaking. To us today that might seem meaningless and perhaps even a deus ex machina, but there is another layer here I found fascinating. Symbolically, we could all find our own Argos, i.e. the history and ancestry of our past, and look there for an answer to be made pure and go forward. Tradition speaks to us today, whether through old heirlooms in a family's possession or through studying history and artifacts from our ancestors.

Looking at how the Argonauts bested the Sirens, it's obvious how important it is to have artists and talent on our side to change the current power dynamics of culture. Orpheus shows the timelessness and power music has on the human and monstrous alike. He could move the gods to tears. The greatest argument for religion is the sublimity that comes from hearing music. Nietzsche, the self-titled antichrist himself, wrote in *Birth of Tragedy* to resist the religious temptation music brings, because of its power and transcendence. It was glorious enough to make the philosopher of power resist its eternal embrace. Even he was wary of the power of the sublime in music and couldn't help but be caught up in its rapture. We need that kind of sublimity and power in our music, especially if we want to get past the Sirens. He drowned them out, and we should do the same to our Sirens of the modern day, i.e. the ones that virtue-signal and hurl insults, shaming people into silence and/or leading them to desert the right side and even embrace the left side, all because of a fear of being judged. Stigmas can be overcome when a man like Orpheus plays beautiful music. Beauty destroys the mob. They tolerate everything but beauty, and if one of us can make music that moves people to tears with courageous nationalistic song, then the Sirens' singing will fall on deaf ears and they will be revealed for what they are—beings that scream the loudest with nothing to say. Those who have an aesthetic and ancestral foundation cannot hear their judgmental lies. Do not forget what the mob truly is. The mob is the rabble, the evil herd who stampedes on what is good and beautiful just to keep up the status quo. There is no beauty in the mob, but there is beauty in one who steps from out of the shadows of the unthinking herd. As long as you are in the mob, you are ugly. Beauty belongs to the tyrant. The mob destroys beauty, but beauty destroys the mob.

The scene where the Argonauts encounter Talos can be interpreted in many different ways, but this is one interpretation I've come up with and am privy to. Let us think of the bronze giant Talos as the average American today. They hurl insults like rocks at whoever drifts from the status quo. Furthermore, Talos could also be represented abstractly as the culture and system generalized. Its bronze casting pretty much guarantees that no new guard will come around, because just like our culture, it seems impenetrable. It is the system that is a capitalistic country run by corporations and banks instead of a goodwill government that wants the best for their people, not the most profit in materialistic gains for a select few. For us to beat a monster such as Talos, we need to be like Medea and calm it. Wearing the mask of politeness and empathy can trick even the stubbornest of enemies into speaking honestly and openly with us. That is when we can interject with little inception-like suggestions that make our enemies think they came up with the dissident view (whatever it might be) themselves. That's how you get to the blood vessel underneath the bronze. It sounds simple but I've actually used this method myself, wearing a mask of agreeableness and asking questions related to their beliefs. Give them a biblical-like allegory and allow them to figure it out and offer an answer. Even the harshest of ideas can be made more palatable that way.

For the last part of this myth, the obvious maxim that you shouldn't trust just anybody is perfect here. But this also shows how monogamy and traditionalism makes for a thriving homelife and society. Jason failed his wife, and that is one of the least heroic and manly things one could do. His impatience in killing Pelias and then

marrying Creusa, daughter of Creon, was what brought
about his downfall. You must be patient! Even bringing
back a treasure like the golden fleece might not be enough
to win over the elites. Think back to Hercules's patience
with his 12 labors. Compare that to Jason and his race for
retribution and vengeance, and even power (in Corinth).
His betrayal of Medea's love and vows angered Hera and
she turned her favor away while Helios helped Medea
escape. The gods were finished with the once-great hero.
Remember that to have connections to higher-up places,
one must be certain to not go too wholly and openly against
their wishes. You earn trust by continuing to bring golden
fleece-like sacrifices and biding your time. What happens
when you turn away from all your allies and look for power
alone? You become Jason, perpetually melancholic and
with nobody by your side. His sad death in his once
glorious and powerful ship is a warning for all. His rotting
ship had become a corpse just like himself. Do not go at
this struggle alone and do not turn you back on allies, no
matter how strenuous and weak the relationship is. Don't
let a glorious past crumble into dust, drowning you along
with it in some distant desert that nobody knows exists.
Remember and move forward in honor of the past.

23
Straight from the Source

Back when I was reading Edith Hamilton and her book on mythology (a basic primer of sorts), I was often left frustrated at her automatic siding with the females as if they were helpless damsels, and her dislike of pure and masculine strength. This is why when studying mythology or history, one must always come to one's own opinions by reading the source material itself. There is always an angle and bias, no matter who is writing it or how correct and fair said writer claims to be. One of the problems I had was her dislike of Hercules and her preference for the much weaker Theseus. She pits the two of them against each other as if they were eternal enemies, and she made it seem like Hercules was some dumb brute and Theseus some enlightened defender of democracy and equality. Very weak of her!

For one thing, Theseus was the kind of character in mythology that would turn up in all kinds of stories, almost always as a background figure unworthy of being the main focus as an alpha male. And to make matters worse, when leading his men in battle, he wouldn't let them loot the cities they'd beaten and receive any reward for their fighting. I'm all for fairness and respectability in war; Napoleon won great respect from the territories he conquered by not allowing his men to rape the women or senselessly destroy (don't get me started on the savagery of Muslim troops who were allowed to do whatever they wanted for a time immediately after conquering a city, in the name of their holy and peaceful god). However, Napoleon was also set on securing valuables and loot for his own nation and museum in Paris. What is Theseus to this? He didn't let his men do a thing, almost as if they hadn't won and suffered at all. Why fight if for no reward?

It is a miracle his men didn't turn on him. His philosophy was not a life-affirming one, that's for certain.

Oh, but he was such a peaceful and loving king that brought cities together! You might say as such, but don't tell me he was greater than Hercules. Athens loved Theseus, the world loved Hercules. Athens with its philosophers was an admirable state, but its lack of military prowess and might is why it never achieved the greatness that Rome reached centuries later. Thinking alone is never enough! Men must act, and say yes to the struggles of life. Theseus only had half the labors Hercules had. He also was only able to kill the Minotaur because it was asleep. Theseus accomplished much and was a great hero in his own right, I'm just frustrated at how he's treated as some modern-day, mythological saint of sorts by our cucked standards of today.

We know of Hercules's might and wit, I don't need to recount them here. However, I wanted to make mention of Edith Hamilton's insult and disagreement with Hercules's willingness to suffer and take on punishment. She called his consistent sacrifice foolhardy and unnecessary. Women recounting heroic deeds should not be trusted. Do you think she would understand a Coriolanus? Do you think she understands honor and the concept of dying for it rather than living with evil and sin gnawing at the heart? Instead she cheers Theseus and his love for his despicable wife Phaedra. She's the same wife who after falling in love with Hippolytus (Theseus's son unrelated to Phaedra) was rejected by him, and out of spite she killed herself and lied in her suicide note, claiming Hippolytus had raped her. The fool Theseus trusted this woman over Hippolytus, his honorable son, who had forsaken all women in pursuit of purity and power in the hunt, serving the chaste Artemis with a similar and fervent chastity.

Hippolytus had shown no reason for such an
accusation to be true, and he had bonded with Theseus over
hunting and strength before all of this. Hippolytus had
shunned the whore Phaedra and her disgusting advances,
and she killed herself out of dishonor and shame, and like a
true wench sought to bring him down with her. Edith
Hamilton cheered Theseus' faithfulness to his deceitful
wife as he called on Poseidon to avenge her, and
Hippolytus was unjustly killed as he fled—by his own
horses, when his chariot overturned (the doing of the gods
who answered Theseus's call for vengeance).

Hippolytus belongs in the volcel hall of fame.
Theseus was his father and his mother was the queen of the
Amazons, Hippolyta. He decided he wanted nothing to do
with women, and served the honorable Artemis. His muscle
and good looks were irresistible, and Phaedra dishonored
herself and him. The parallels with today are many, as a
woman can claim whatever she wants about a man and she
will be believed and the man maligned. Perhaps us
powerful men are better off cultivating our strength in the
forest. It is interesting that in Roman mythology,
Hippolytus became the god of the forest named Virbius.
This is interesting, as in this version of the myth, he
spurned Aphrodite for Artemis and the jealous goddess
made Phaedra fall in love with him for revenge (only
somewhat excusing Phaedra, still a despicable liar in the
end). Artemis then asked Asclepius, the god of medicine, to
resurrect him. Thus, he became Virbius and reigned
proudly as a volcel god dedicated to becoming more
powerful and righteous than his soft father Theseus ever
could have been. Incels, take note, as women like
Aphrodite cannot be trusted! Read Edith Hamilton's whiny
mythology to see what I mean. Hercules is the greatest hero
of all, and not some dumb brute. He's too manly and proud
for the typical old woman to comprehend.

With Edith Hamilton in mind, let us consider the woman issue. It is no small coincidence that evil came from Eve in the Bible, and from Pandora in Greek mythology. Women syphon the masculine and will not stop until the blood of heroes is sucked dry, and only soyboy skeletons will be left to clatter about. The current path is leading to this castrated future; as heroic men we must tyrannize the sissy fits and femboys. We must display our strength. As crazy as the modern woman has become, she cannot resist the purely masculine. After all, Aphrodite came from Heaven's penis, and Eve from Adam's rib. True and powerful beauty is masculine. Adam was created first and only received the helper Eve because he was too weak and complained. Created in a state of perfection, Adam could not bear the responsibility of tyranny of himself and the earth he had been charged to cultivate. Man needed a helper after all. We live with the feminine in our midst, and it has taken on a unique beauty of its own—the feminine and the masculine complementing each other into a fullness rivaling divinity, when the two are made one in holy matrimony or through well-formed and serious erotic relations.

I will not command a woman to not work, nor to forego becoming intelligent and fit. All these are good things that should be pursued by man and woman alike. Some women are not fit to be mothers. Some women are meant to be Athena, warring like Joan of Arc without the thought of man but only that of the glory of a nation and people. Some women are meant to be Artemis, hunting and providing for the weak like a lioness providing for her own. The key word is some. Yet the highest calling of a woman is not to be like man, for a man is naturally stronger and advantaged in the work requiring physical prowess (and that is not to say women cannot become strong like an above average man, but there is an obvious biological reason that WNBA players barely dunk, and the best one couldn't defeat the worst NBA player). Women's minds work differently and that can be an advantage in areas dominated by men simply through bringing a different perspective. But all these cases are the few, and too many women today are shamed for fulfilling the holy role of motherhood.

Man is meant to be Heaven, watching over the feminine Earth who holds her children close to her bosom. The perfect woman, the ultimate example, can be found in the Holy Theotokos—the Mother of God, Mary. She held the most powerful being ever close to her bosom. She fed and clothed him, her womb like the ark of the covenant containing a power and glory that would envelop and destroy anyone else. And for my Protestant readers who seek to diminish her or pretend she was unimportant, what was Christ's first miracle? She commanded him to turn water into wine. That's what women should strive for—to raise powerful children. Hiring someone else to watch over your children is a travesty that impedes development and greatness. How could you trust some uneducated fool to influence your child? Your child! The one who came from your loins, who dwelled inside you! Women, motherhood is a divine calling that is more valuable than perhaps any other. At least in Christianity, the greatest human being outside of Christ was his mother. Choose your vocation wisely and do not let the wine aunts and lonely harpies shame you. Their ovaries are dried up, they are alone and undesirable. If they were so happy, why do they feel the need to shout down young mothers with glowing skin and beautiful families? They have their cats, you have your kin.

One woman in Greek mythology who is almost always portrayed as one of these jealous old bags (despite having many children of her own) is the queen of Olympus herself, Hera. She is always nagging Zeus, even if he doesn't deserve it (although I must say he frequently does, but that is another matter,) and curses any woman he looks at twice. She frequently seeks to kill his children that he had with other woman, not caring if his seed is just an infant or child. A violent she-wolf, the evils she poured out on valiant Hercules are unrivaled in terms of their harshness and severity. But not to dwell only on the Hercules myth, I want to instead look at Io and how she so ruthlessly cursed the poor woman.

Zeus characteristically fell for Io because of her beauty, and the wrath of the ice queen Hera soon poured forth on the unsuspecting girl. To protect her from Hera, Zeus turned her into a cow. Real manly! Need I remind you all why I prefer to be considered a Titan rather than an Olympian god? Regardless of the disguise, Hera did the most feminist thing she could: she sent a terrible gadfly to buzz and nibble at Io in her heifer form endlessly—just like women of the left today endlessly gripe and moan about the patriarchy, like gnats gnawing at the system that has been reshaped in their image of weakness. Women are not discriminated against! The only discrimination comes from the feminists against men, and the traditional women that are glad to be loving mothers. There is no love in women like this, they are all Heras torturing the beautiful out of a jealousy and misery that they refuse to admit exists. They curse all and claim to be perfect, accusing anyone of hatred who doesn't find their flaws beautiful. You cannot make a flaw into an asset in the game of attraction—if you are fat you are not attractive! If you don't wash your hair, or if you dye it into looking like cotton candy, then real men will want nothing to do with you.

For men, we need more than just to be alone with only our significant other. If unlucky enough to be latched together with a Hera (whether by your own fault or your partner's devolution), a group of good men by your side

157

means the world. Find manly comrades to struggle with, to battle against, and to sharpen your wits and strength as iron clashing against iron. Your wife should be your best friend, if you have one. Yet, the Holy Trinity is male and the 12 apostles were also male. I stated already that the best human besides Christ was his mother, but at the same time he chose men to lead his flock. Men carry a strength and vigor that cannot be matched by women, at least not in the same manner. You tell me, would you fight a woman as you would a man? Chivalry exists for a reason. Seek a band of men, become brothers and put skin in the game together. That is how you can experience the fullness of life.

For the most meaningful and pleasurable existence on this earth to be had, we must all learn to participate in the feminine and the masculine, on both sides. If taking on the worthy mantle of being a volcel, do not neglect the feminine either (or vice versa if a female with masculine). The beauty of Mother Earth, the eternal Gaia can only be seen with the light of fatherly Heaven spreading his arms above. It is not good for man to be alone. Go and seek the power of both, experiencing and creating beauty that expresses the whole of humanity. That is the calling we nationalists must take up. Choose the role that best suits your strength, and do not let someone else shame you away from living for an eternal beauty.

24
The Ironic Oppressor

The delicious irony of sitting in a social justice graduate school class required by the university is that everything I do in the future will be to subvert their nefarious goals of making unequal people equal without merit (making the powerful weak and the weak average). I will be the one spreading the glorious truth of tyranny as a good. If they want me to speak in terms of power and be inclusive, I will be as offensively powerful as I can be and highlight the glorious history of my forefathers. Many people in my class, at least at first, thought that the social justice inclusivity nonsense was just that—nonsense! A class supposed to be teaching us to teach, taught us only how to be taught by unqualified minorities. We spent a whole 4-hour class session on the good of immigration. Illegal or not, they espoused immigration as only good without negatives. Seemingly every statement made in supposed scholarly texts in these classes are based on feeling instead of fact.

My school is in a conservative area of the country, yet little do the locals know that leftist extremism is being espoused as the norm under the guise of progress and education. These students end up polluting two of the most influential areas of culture: media and teaching. Our children are indoctrinated with these lies 24/7, unless we keep a close eye on them (which is why stay-at-home moms are so crucial in a society lacking traditional values and guidance).

I don't want to sound too defeatist or alarmist though, as there are other viable forms of education. The Montessori method is very interesting and has been proven to be very effective. It teaches children to be independent and learn through trial and error on their own. Dr.

Montessori was an Italian Catholic woman who brought her method to the streets of Italy to help the poor. Unfortunately, many Montessori schools are now filled with rich leftist babies who whine if they don't get their way. Likewise, many teachers in the system have a sociology degree and rainbow-colored hair. Caution should be had, but there is only so much brainwashing that can be done in a Montessori school because the curriculum is standard and the teacher is an observer instead of a pontificator. If that is unavailable, home-schooling is best, but I understand that is not doable for many of you. Worst case is that our children are forced into the public school system. If that is the only option, then we have to equip our children and the next generations with as much information as possible so they are best prepared to deal with the rampant nihilism and degeneracy that infects so much of the education system and society as a whole.

I also had to take a diversity class (and am currently taking another one—these are all mandatory) where things were stated and accepted as fact without any evidence other than feelings and shouting accusations of racism backing it up. My professor with a doctorate in education said her goal is to make the white students feel guilty. Her words, not mine. She told us that because we are white, we are racist and privileged, no matter what. Even the homeless white man has more privilege than LeBron James. Statements like those had my classmates fuming. Yet, as the insults and offences piled up, my classmates have all begun to turn in the name of inclusivity. Really, I just don't think they can stomach being called racist, and they just want to feel liked. Almost all of them have been broken under the weight of the equality myth. There are no tyrants in my class but myself and I grin and laugh as they seethe in hatred of themselves.

We are being taught to stop being white oppressors. Little do they realize such inflammatory and unbalanced accusations have made me want to oppress them even more. My tyrant heart beats all the quicker as they fuel the power inside me with the will to dominate these imbeciles who ironically seek to dominate me for being different, but not in the "right way". These are the kind of people that should be thrown into a psych ward. Here is all you need to glean from such pathetic displays: keep getting better as the herd weakens itself with lolling stupidity to the incessant tune of false guilt. The only ones guilty are those who choose to be weak.

I've now become a part of the education system and am working on seizing control from within. I'm already a cog and am being refitted as a spout. Once I'm the one releasing steam as I please, only then can I become the wrench that tightens and loosens the system's bolts as I see fit. Infiltration is essential.

25
Goddess
Rangabes Part III of III

He strode triumphant into his city with his hand clutching the feathers, his face and stature assured with vigor and strength. A year he'd been gone but Justinian still towered triumphant and Hagia Sophia held her glory high. The Ottomans could come! Not worried at being reprimanded for his absence, he knew that the weakened military of old Byzantium was desperate for heroes such as he. If the captains refused to welcome him back, he would prove his worth and honor through dueling. The Emperor could oversee it himself! But that could wait. He must find the beautiful Venia. He'd found her myth and conquered it.

Hustling outside the palace courtyards and in the shade of the great church, he searched for her sultry form. Sure enough, as if he'd never left, she stood there in her glory, the same wispy green dress hanging enchantingly off her divine flesh. Her tanned skin glowed as if the sun had caressed her once, and never let go since. If the Greek and Roman myths of old were true, she'd be of divine stock, without a doubt. With his besting of Tengri who'd turned out to be none other than Sirius, he wouldn't have been surprised if those ancient civilizations had been on to something. The Blessed Virgin forgive him, but could Mt. Olympus stand true in all ages, even with the Lord towering above as always? He didn't know, but the question had plagued him his entire uneventful return home. With no signs from any more gods, he had to remind himself that the feathers and fangs in his possession were true.

"My Rangabes." She strode over to him with all the refinement of a queen and stared up into his face with both her hands clutching at his lengthy, curled black beard.

"Travel certainly has touched you. When's the last time you shaved?" She sniffed and playfully backed away. "Or bathed?"

"Tengri was real. The Dog Star," he muttered, lowering his head and looking away. He scratched at his cheeks only just realizing how beggarly he must look. The matter of myths existing had understandably taken precedence in his mind. Besides, he no longer trusted Turkish inns.

Venia's brow furrowed and she smirked. "Your pockets bulge, and is that my dagger in your other hand that you clutch so tight." She laughed and swept forward and peered into his eyes, her lively aroma choking out his dead one. "Was my gift your glory?" Her questions were teasing answers in themselves. She reached into his pockets, lingering there before plucking the feathers and fangs out but leaving the dagger for him to keep.

"Venia... the myths are real. What does that mean now, when the ancient has been forgotten?" he asked as she stepped back and he stood there confused.

"My Rangabes... How I wish I could call you mine as I once did with worthy Anchises. But you are no Roman or Ancient Greek, my Byzantine friend. Your city will die in the years to come and you with it. When you are plunged into the depths and at the feet of patient Pluto and Proseperina, do not forget Venia who opened your eyes to the heroic mythical realms of being. You've faced pretend gods, and you now know that what was once alive is dormant in a weak and sleepy race of moderns. It will worsen, it must. But I refuse to cower in the skin of some sheep. I will not slither with the old gods. Aeneas was born to me. And another will be born again, yet not from me." She paused and looked longingly at the sky. Her eyes had misted like a swamp on a starlit night. She was not looking at Rangabes or the people around her, but at something distant. "There is another womb who will bring greatness and glory worthy of ancient heroes! You, Rangabes, you my sad, suffering soldier, will not long from now die a forgotten hero when your city inevitably falls. But you will ascend from Pluto's realm riding the back of the slumbering Cerberus, the hound of Death once more waking to his old call. Ascend and return to me then. Your resurrection will be rewarded with eternity. You might not know it, but when great Constantine spread Rome's wings to the east, he brought your namesake with him. From his eagle's plumage, you Rangabes breathe with the lungs of Caesar Augustus. I see my Aeneas in you, however distant that mythic past. Greatness will be born from your loins once more. But you must suffer for much longer. You must overcome and become worthy of your ancestors. With Cerberus as your steed, you may return."

Venia's irises twisted like vortexes, sucking him in with her talk and look of glory. She glided up to his face, her nose nearly brushing his and she blew a breath of perfume too divine to describe, and his eyes rolled back into his skull as her true name massaged the frightened neurons of his brain.

Venus. Venus. Venus.

Her divine name blackened his consciousness and when he awoke, she was nowhere to be found. He searched his pockets for the feathers and fangs and found nothing. A fever dream, none of it real. But then, a sharp pointed dagger pressed his finger. His heart soared as he clutched the strange dagger to his breast. He would never forget her promise and he'd heed her call, dead or alive. He would follow the trail of the mythic, to taste the fountains of glory that the eternal heroic found worthy to feed. He would not forget, and he would strive. Venus required it.

26
The Sixth Age

Heroic does not mean good. Heroic means power used wisely. What is power used wisely? It is power that serves the collective; it is a sacrificial power that seeks the glory of those worth dying for. Being heroic is to be a tyrant, dominating your lesser parts with discipline and rewarding glory with splendor. The tyrant of tomorrow is a hero of his people. For such a tyrant, his people come first, as they are his everything. If all tyrants as such existed in each nation, the world would become heroic in the mythical sense as it was when only the Titans ruled.

Hesiod establishes in his classic *Works and Days* the five ages of man, in which he explains the different ages of humanity and its development (of course mythically). The Golden Age was the first age of humans, when Kronos was still on the throne. The humans of this age lived amongst the gods, with harmony and beauty in every shining face. They were kind, noble and lived in a time of pure peace. The people of this age were so pure that they became guardians of spirit and lived on through their love.

The Silver Age was not all that different than the Golden Age except that the people of this era lived 100 years as children (or perhaps in childlike innocence) before aging and dying soon after. Typically, the children would grow and then all the sudden be at enmity with one another as soon as adulthood struck. Kronos' defeat at the hands of Zeus marked the beginning of this age. The men of this age were blasphemous and refused to worship the deities, so Zeus ultimately wiped them out. The people of this age became spirits in the Underworld instead of the free roaming spirts of the Golden Age folk on earth.

The third age is the Bronze Age. It was an age of power and bravado. These men were all fashioned from the ash tree. Almost everything was made of bronze, from the houses to the armor and seemingly everything in between. Because they were so violent and cruel, their spirits did not linger. They forever dwell in Hades with no hope of ever leaving. The end of this age was brought about by the great flood of Deucalion, which drowned them all.

IV   The Heroic age is the fourth age, and definitely the most robust one. Most of the well-known heroes of Greek antiquity lived during this time. The Argonauts' quest for the golden fleece, the Odyssey, the Trojan War and the 12 labors of Hercules took place during this time. The worthy of this race of people died and live in Elysium, the paradise in the midst of Hades that only those of great heroism and power could live in.   V

The last of the five ages is the Iron Age, which is the age we still find ourselves in today. This age is a miserable one compared to the first four. People are in constant despair and pain; death is commonplace, even to those who are in apparent good health. Hesiod decried the wickedness and evil of the age because nobody felt shame for their evils. The majority is degenerate, and the gods have forsaken humanity to its lot in this age, no longer helping fight against evil because there is now evil in every heart.

This Age of Iron today I fear is in many ways much worse than it was back in Hesiod's time (600 BC). This age seems to have no end in sight. And if this age were to miraculously end, would a new one arise or would we return to a past age? I know you Anarcho-Prims would love a return to the Golden Age, an age that was said to be agrarian and peaceful with no need for war or technology. If a return were possible, I'd look to the Heroic Age, which should come as no surprise. People lived and died in that age as much, if not more so than they do now, but great men and women were plentiful, accomplishing feats that make popular athletes of today seem like children. Even the often-overlooked Silver Age would be much better than today. Long lives followed by intense bursts of power once childhood is left behind. Strife was relegated to those who grew into it, and all eventually did. The Silver Age could be looked at as one long life of preparation for a powerful finish and a burst of an ecstatic lust for life. An intriguing concept that is far removed from our Iron Age.

I wonder if BAP would prefer the Bronze Age? It would be fitting, and the pure manliness and will to power on display in that age were not even matched by the Heroic Age. If you wanted to live in an age that allowed you to dominate, and encouraged the exercise of will and absolute power, the Bronze Age is the age for you. It is the age of acquiring space for yourself and man-spreading across the globe, smiting any who dare question your authority. It might seem odd to say, but I would prefer that age to ours now. Bronze is a much stronger metal than the plastic we surround ourselves with today. The Iron Age might as well be called the Plastic Age in modern times, while still meaning the same thing as it did then. Women and men hide from the world in houses and rooms removed from nature and strife. The suffering of today is more mental than physical, especially in the wealthy Western countries. Lack of meaning, listlessness, and a general ennui plague most and they try to cure it by filling the emptiness with meaningless toys and trends. There is no skin in the game. There is no risk. Instead of becoming Nietzsche's Übermensch and building on the slopes of Vesuvius, we've leveled the volcano and covered it with a concrete office building that has a nice little coffee shop attached.

We can learn from the past and emulate the great heroes of old. However, an age that has passed us is gone and any attempt at recreating it is mere roleplaying and inauthentic to the will to life and power. So then, what do

we do with our age of Iron/Plastic? We recycle. We take
the good from now and take the good from old, and make
our own good that does not yet exist. The good I speak of is
what is powerful and meaningful for the individual as a
member of the whole. If every nation serves their own
nation's best interest, a combination of the Bronze and
Heroic Ages might just be formed. Do not roll your eyes, it
is not as far-fetched as it sounds. People are tiring of crazy
leftists claiming gender isn't real and biology is false.
Leftism is a cult of degeneracy and weakness. To combat
such cultural decay, a powerful right wing will form in
rebellion.

Trump is the beginning. We powerful tyrants of
tomorrow are the future. Then a new age will begin, one
where nationhood is sacred and peoples and cultures are
respected and cared for. Greatness will be encouraged and
democracy finished. In this age, power will be rewarded
and the strong will care for their own first. Whether it be
through Fascism, Monarchy, a Republic, or some unknown
form that has yet to be created—the age to come will be
one worthy of mythological heroes, and new ones will arise
all around the globe. The stars will then be reached and
dangerous exploration encouraged. This new age will be
called the Alloy Age. Alloy is when two metals are fused
together to bring greater strength than even the most
powerful pure metals alone. A fitting name for an age that
will combine the best facets of the heroic old and create
and discover new methods of glory. Combining the two
will lead to an unbreakable age of power. This is the
glorious future I long for. This is why I am writing this
manifesto. The mythic heroes both real and fabled offer us
shining examples to follow, and we must combine their
strength with our time of technology and knowledge. Be
glorious and powerful! Who knows, this new age might
soon be at hand.

27
Ascend Olympus

The degeneracy of today is toxic and fuming. It is difficult to avoid breathing the air, but we must turn our backs and ascend the mountain towards the clear, life-affirming heavens. We tyrants of tomorrow have an advantage, as we are always becoming greater while the masses continue stewing in their slime. Degeneracy to domination, that is the transformation only we can bring about. With minds of steel and bodies of sculpted marble, we must dominate the degenerates to bring about the cleansing fires of the Alloy Age. Steel bound to titanium, the present fused to the heroic past. Only we tyrants can make the mythic become actuality; then the mythic heroic man that is unthinkable to modernity as it is now will arise and take back his rightful place in power. Nations will become nations again. Death will not be hidden away. Truth will flood the streets and wipe away the slimy and filthy lies left behind.

It starts with tyrannizing yourself and becoming unbreakable in mind, body and spirit. Then infiltration. As our movement blossoms and positions of power are taken by us tyrants, the real change can start to begin. For now, we must be patient like Hercules working through each labor without complaint and with longsuffering faith in his own greatness. Alliances will be forged. Good comrades of our own will certainly fall. But in the end, it is the tyrant of tomorrow that will stand tall, for his tyranny is the kind that can never be extinguished, for to him—tomorrow is today and vice versa.

We are always becoming, and this becoming will be the leftist degenerates' undoing. Let us do the doing. Let us leave the depths of Tartarus and take back Olympus. The gods have vanished, and there are no true men of power at the top. It is vacant, waiting for power and greatness to return to its rightful place. Stay tyrannical, friends! Tomorrow is ours when today it begins. Begin your ascent. I will see you there.

Made in the USA
Monee, IL
15 May 2021